Grammar Essentials for Proofreading, Copyediting & Business Writing

Boost Your Writing Skills

Ashan R. Hampton

Cornerstone Publishing
Arkansas

D0880485

Published by Cornerstone Communications & Publishing, Little Rock, Arkansas.

For bulk orders and discounts, call 1-844-212-0689. Check www.lulu.com for coupon codes.

Cover Design: Ashan R. Hampton
Cover photo: © Can Stock Photo / mast3r

Websites: www.arhampton.com
www.onyxedonline.com

Library of Congress Control Number: 2018905738
ISBN-13: 978-1-387-91413-5

Printed in the United States of America.

First Edition.

Cataloging-in-Publication Data is on file with the Library of Congress.

10 9 8 7 6 5 4 3 2 1

About the Author

Ashan R. Hampton has worked as an English instructor in higher education for over 20 years, most notably at Morehouse College in Atlanta, Georgia. She is also a proud graduate of the *Donaghey Scholars Program* at the University of Arkansas at Little Rock under the direction of Dr. C. Earl Ramsey, Emeritus.

Ashan's original research, *History of the Arkansas State Hospital 1859-1930*, was published in the *Pulaski County Historical Review* (1995), and continues to be cited by history scholars today. Her articles on notable African American Arkansans also appear in the *Encyclopedia of Arkansas History and Culture*.

With her doctoral studies on hold, Ashan has found success in online education. She produces and teaches her own writing and grammar courses for global audiences through her company, *Onyx Online Education & Training*. Ashan is also a published author, digital media producer, proofreader and copyeditor.

Visit her website: **www.arhampton.com**.

Contents

Grammar Essentials Pre-Test

Complete all of the questions to the best of your ability before peeking at the answers at the end of this assessment. Good luck and happy learning!

✓ 1. __Noun__ Names a person, place, thing or idea.

✗ 2. __pronoun__ Describes or modifies a verb or adjective.

✓ 3. __Verb__ Suggests action or state of being.

4. Karen is saving money to buy a new air conditioner.

✓   (a) complete sentence

     b. fragment

5. Gives the user a painful shock.

✓   a. comma splice

     (b.) fragment

6. The mayor has a previous engagement, the meeting must be postponed.

✓   a. run-on

     (b.) comma splice

7. My cat often_____the mail carrier.

✓   a. chase

     (b.) chases

8. Everyone must bring_____own chair to the outdoor jazz concert.

    a. their

    b. his or her

9. The cab driver told Vic and_____that traffic on the bridge was heavy at this time of day.

    a. me

    b. I

10. Having watched the movie closely, the ending was confusing.

    a. dangling modifier

    b. misplaced modifier

11. Plump sausages, the dinner guests looked forward to the main course.

    a. dangling modifier

    b. misplaced modifier

12. When LeBron dunked the ball into the net, the fans _____wild.

    a. go

    b. went

13. Jana took twenty-four selfies in two minutes.

    a. active voice

    b. passive voice

Answers on back of page.

Answers: *Pre-Test*

1. noun ✓

2. adverb ✗

3. verb ✓

4. a ✓

5. b ✓

6. b ✓

7. b ✓

8. b ✗

9. a ✓

10. a ✓

11. b ✓

12. b ✓

13. a ✓

Chapter One

Sentence Fragments

Photo Credit: © Thinkstockphotos, Thomas Northcut.

What is a Fragment?

A **sentence fragment** does not express a complete thought. Although a fragment could contain a subject and a verb, the sentence omits important information. The missing part makes the sentence sound unfinished or strange. Since fragments are unclear, you must fill in the missing words or phrases to correct the sentence and to relieve the reader's frustration.

Example: Fell to the ground.

In the above example, more information is required to make the action of the sentence clear to the reader. What fell to the ground?

Who or what is the subject? If someone spoke this sentence to you and stopped talking, you would immediately start asking questions as a natural need for clarity.

Correction:

- Ashan's corndog fell to the ground.

Even Better:

- Ashan's footlong corndog, drenched in mustard, rolled off the picnic table at the state fair and fell to the ground.

Correcting Fragments

- Follow **basic sentence structure** by including a subject, a verb, and descriptive clauses and phrases to complete the meaning of a sentence.
- Read your writing out loud. Generally, it is easier to **hear** missing words than to **see** them on a printed page or computer screen.
- Find the true, simple **subject** of the sentence.
- Find the true, simple **verb** of the sentence.

Examples:

- Just three days.
- We have **just three days** to move into our new apartment.

- Works at the front desk.
- Robert **works at the front desk** of the hotel.

- Leaving the office before noon.
- Our manager will be **leaving the office before noon** today.

- Make money on social media.
- Instead of working a job, Olivia wants to **make money on social media**.

Fragments Exercise

Directions: Write **complete sentence** or **fragment** in the space provided.

1. _____C_____ Since Jean was not at the meeting, I took notes in her absence.

2. _____F_____ When my cousin moved to Dallas, Texas, after he graduated.

3. _____F_____ Regina forgot.

4. _____F_____ The largest source of revenue for the organization.

5. _____C_____ Larry deserves great praise and recognition for his teamwork.

6. _____C_____ Before you leave, get your parking pass validated.

7. _____F_____ Is an important part of a healthy lifestyle.

Answers: Fragments Exercise

1. complete sentence

2. fragment

3. complete sentence

4. fragment

5. complete sentence

6. complete sentence

7. fragment

Chapter Two
Run-on Sentences

Photo Credit: © Pexels.com, Fauxels.

What is a Run-on?

A **run-on** consists of two or more complete sentences joined together with no punctuation separating them. Run-on sentences are also called **fused sentences**.

Example:

- Henry and Rose are both in their late thirties they decided to pay for their own wedding. *and*

Explanation: In this example, the first complete sentence ends with the word "thirties." The second sentence begins with "they." Notice that no period ends the first sentence, and no semicolon is used to properly connect these two short sentences.

Correcting Run-ons:

1. Make two complete sentences.
2. Use a comma and a coordinating conjunction.
3. Use a semicolon.
4. Use a subordinating conjunction with proper punctuation.

Original Example:

- Henry and Rose are both in their late thirties they decided to pay for their own wedding.

Correction #1:

- Henry and Rose are both in their late **thirties. They** decided to pay for their own wedding.

Correction #2:

- Henry and Rose are both in their late thirties, **so** they decided to pay for their own wedding.

Correction #3:

- Henry and Rose are both in their late thirties**; they** decided to pay for their own wedding.

Semicolon

Correction #4:

- **Since** Henry and Rose are both in their late **thirties, they** decided to pay for their own wedding.

For more on how to **correct run-on sentences**, see *"Adult Learner Grammar Essentials."* Get yours at **www.arhampton.com**.

Run-on Exercise

Directions: Identify each sentence as a **run-on** or a **complete sentence**. Write the correct answer in the space provided.

1. ___R___ Shop once a week stick to a preplanned grocery list.

2. ___C___ Dorothy Woods won the Business Woman of the Year award from the Junior League.

3. ___C___ D'Andre applied for a small business loan to open a barbershop.

4. ___C___ Using real butter is the key to baking great potato skins.

5. ___R___ Concert pianists must practice six to eight hours a day they are so dedicated and ambitious.

6. ___R___ Concussions are a huge problem in football too many players are suffering.

7. ___C___ Marsha started a blog for natural health, but her writing is terrible.

Answers: Run-on Exercise

1. run-on

2. complete sentence

3. complete sentence

4. complete sentence

5. run-on

6. run-on

7. complete sentence

Chapter Three
Comma Splice

Photo Credit: © Pexels.com, Christina Morillo.

What is a Comma Splice?

A **comma splice** occurs when two complete sentences are separated by a comma instead of a period or a semicolon. In addition to being a grammar error, comma splices also create punctuation errors, since the wrong type of punctuation is used to separate sentences. Comma splices are also called **comma faults**.

Example:

- Rhemona recently opened a photography studio, she still works full-time as a dental hygienist.

Explanation: In this example, the first complete sentence is separated from the second sentence by a comma instead of a period. The first sentence ends with "studio," and the second sentence begins with "she."

Correcting Comma Splices:

1. Make two complete sentences.
2. Use a comma and a coordinating conjunction.
3. Use a semicolon.
4. Use a subordinating conjunction with proper punctuation.

Original Example:

- Rhemona recently opened a photography studio, she still works full-time as a dental hygienist.

Correction #1:

- Rhemona recently opened a photography **studio. She** still works full-time as a dental hygienist.

Correction #2:

- Rhemona recently opened a photography **studio, but** she still works full-time as a dental hygienist.

Correction #3:

- Rhemona recently opened a photography **studio; she** still works full-time as a dental hygienist.

Correction #4:

- **Although** Rhemona recently opened a photography **studio,** she still works full-time as a dental hygienist.

NOTE: Comma splices are **corrected** in the **same** way as **run-on** sentences.

For more on how to correct **comma splices**, see *"Adult Learner Grammar Essentials"* at **www.arhampton.com**.

Comma Splice Exercise

Directions: Circle the correct answer below.

1. Veronica's sister served as her doula, she wanted no one else at the birth.

   ✓ **a. comma splice**   **b. correct**

2. Joe Biden will enter the 2020 presidential race.

   a. comma splice   ✓ **b. correct**

3. Mr. Myles claims he is sixty-eight, he is actually seventy-three.

   ✗ (**a. comma splice**)   ✓ **b. correct**

4. The conference rooms are small and lack amenities, but the hotel is lovely and the staff is courteous.

   ✗ ✓ **a. comma splice**   **b. correct**

5. McClellan High School is low performing, the school board refuses to close it.

   ✓ **a. comma splice**   **b. correct**

6. Christmas decorations are available, Thanksgiving is still a month away.

   ✓ **a. comma splice**   **b. correct**

7. Two diabetic parents tend to produce diabetic children.

   a. comma splice   ✓ **b. correct**

Answers: Comma Splice Exercise

1. a

2. b

3. a

4. b

5. a

6. a

7. b

Chapter Four
Subject-Verb Agreement

Photo Credit: © Thinkstockphotos, Ablestock.

What is Subject-Verb Agreement?

Maintaining **subject-verb agreement** means that the number of the subject matches the number of the verb. Basically, a singular subject agrees with a singular verb. The same is true for plural subjects and plural verbs. They both must match.

Example #1:

Eileen walks three miles per day.

Eileen = Subject

- **Eileen** = singular subject
- **walks** = singular verb

Example #1: *(Cont'd)*

- **Eileen walks** three miles per day.
  Ⓢ   Ⓥ

Explanation: In this sentence, Eileen is the subject. Eileen is only one person. Therefore, the verb that describes her actions must also be singular. A singular subject needs a singular verb.

Example #2:

- High school **principals meets** twice a year to discuss district policies.

Correction:

- High school **principals meet** twice a year to discuss district policies.
  Ⓟ   Ⓟ

Explanation: The subject, **principals**, is plural. The verb **meet** is plural, because it has no "–s" on the end, as with singular verbs. Remember, in this example, the plural subject "principals" must match the plural verb "meet" to maintain correct subject-verb agreement.

she — sees Ⓢ
they — see Ⓟ

Rules for Subject-Verb Agreement:

- The subject and the verb must agree in number.

- Singular subjects match and agree with singular verbs.

- Plural subjects match and agree with plural verbs.

Examples:

Incorrect: The choir ride the church bus to the competition.
Correct: The **choir rides** the church bus to the competition.

Incorrect: Ashley Kae creates original paintings and sing beautifully.
Correct: **Ashley Kae creates** original paintings and **sings** beautifully.

Incorrect: My cousin Kevin work as a construction supervisor.
Correct: My cousin **Kevin works** as a construction supervisor.

For more on **subject-verb agreement**, see *"Adult Learner Grammar Essentials"* at **www.arhampton.com.**

Subject–Verb Agreement Exercise

Directions: Circle the correct answer below.

1. The candidate's record on health-care reform is what_____Margaret.

    a. impress
    b. impresses ✓

2. Carrots and sweet potatoes_____vitamin A to the body.

    a. furnish ✓
    b. furnishes

3. My puppy often_____the mail carrier.

    a. chase
    b. chases ✓

4. Ray, along with two of his friends, _plans_ to visit Miami.

    a. plans ✗
    b. plan

5. The planes on the runway_____the taxiway to the terminal.

    a. follows
    b. follow ✓

6. Derrick_____the flaws in the board's plans.

    a. pinpoint
    b. pinpoints ✓

7. John and his coworkers_____the mail each day.

    a. check ✓
    b. checks

Answers: Subject-Verb Agreement Exercise

1. impresses **(b)**

2. furnish **(a)**

3. chases **(b)**

4. plans **(a)**

5. follow **(b)**

6. pinpoints **(b)**

7. check **(a)**

Chapter Five
Dangling & Misplaced Modifiers

Photo Credit: Thinkstock Photos, Digital Vision.

What is a Modifier?

A **modifier** is a word or phrase that describes something. The modifier must be positioned close to whatever it is describing to avoid confusion.

What is a Dangling Modifier?

When a modifier is not properly attached to a subject, (or whatever it is describing within the sentence), it is called a dangling modifier. Dangling modifiers are also called **dangling participles**, because they usually begin with an *-ing* gerund. An error occurs when the modifier phrase is separated from the noun it describes in a way that makes the sentence confusing.

dangling modifier
= dangling participles

Example:

> Coming around the bend in the road, the church was seen.

- Did the **church** come around the bend?

- Did a **person** come around the bend and see the church?

Explanation: Dangling modifiers can be tricky to detect, because readers often supply meaning that is not actually apparent in the sentence, as written.

You might be tempted to assume that a person came around the bend and saw a church. However, the above example lacks a subject, or an actual person to perform the action.

Correction:

- Coming around the bend in the road, **Cara saw the church**.

Now, it is clear that Cara, a person, performed the action in the sentence: *came around the bend and saw the church.*

- However, further revision can clarify the action even more: **Did Cara walk or drive around the bend?**

Revision:

- While driving around the bend in the road, Cara saw the small, country church not far from her grandparents' farm.

Summary: With the above example, you have now learned to correct a dangling modifier, and to add descriptive details for sentence variety and increased clarity.

How to Correct Dangling Modifiers:

- A **dangling modifier** is corrected by moving the phrase close to the noun (person, place or thing) it is describing.

- Secondly, the **subject**—or the performer of the action—must be clear.

What is a Misplaced Modifier?

When the modifier is not close to the word or phrase it describes, the resulting sentence can be ambiguous or even humorous. Therefore, the incorrectly positioned modifier is misplaced.

Example:

- The manager issued a laptop to the assistant with removable storage.

Did the assistant have removable storage?

The manager issued a laptop with removable storage to the assist.

Explanation:

The phrase "with removable storage" is positioned right next to the word "assistant," so the phrase actually describes or modifies the assistant. This phrase is considered misplaced, because the **laptop** logically contains removable storage, not the person—the assistant.

Correction:

modifier (or descriptive phrase)

- The manager issued a laptop **with removable storage** to the assistant.

Notice that the misplaced modifier is technically a prepositional phrase. Move the misplaced modifier next to the word "laptop" to clarify the intended meaning of the sentence.

How to Correct Misplaced Modifiers:

- Move the modifying phrase—(or the descriptive phrase)—close to the subject or the noun that is being described.

What is a Squinting Modifier?

Squinting modifiers are similar to misplaced modifiers, because they are not clearly positioned next to their intended subjects. Squinting modifiers are usually adverbs that can modify a noun, verb, or phrase that precedes it or follows it, which causes confusion for the reader.

Example #1:

- Soul cycling rapidly strengthens your leg muscles.

Does **"rapidly"** modify **"soul cycling"** or **"strengthens"**?

Corrections:

- Soul cycling at a rapid pace strengthens your leg muscles.

- Soul cycling strengthens your leg muscles rapidly.

Example #2:

- Seeing the children running quickly made the teacher lose her temper.

Does **"quickly"** modify **"children running"** or **"lose her temper"**?

Corrections:

- Seeing the children running made the teacher quickly lose her temper.

- Seeing the children running so quickly made the teacher lose her temper.

Dangling & Misplaced Modifier Exercise

Directions: Identify each sentence as correct, a dangling modifier or a misplaced modifier by writing **C, DM**, OR **MM** in the blank.

X 1. __MM__ Containing tennis courts and pools, some hotels are more like resorts. C

X 2. __C__ Having watched the movie closely, the ending was confusing. DM

X 3. __MM__ Viewing alcohol as a beverage, it is often not considered a drug. DM

4. __C__ Before the meeting began, Matt and Thomas photocopied the agenda and placed one in each chair. ✓

X 5. __DM__ Plump sausages, the dinner guests looked forward to the main course. MM

X 6. __MM__ Soaring over the treetops in a hot air balloon, the view was spectacular. DM

7. __MM__ Powered by hydrogen, the engineers designed a new kind of car. ✓

Answers: Dangling & Misplaced Modifier Exercise

1. C

2. DM

3. DM

4. C

5. MM

6. DM

7. MM

Chapter Six
Capitalization

Photo Credit: Thinkstock Photos, Creatas Images.

What is Capitalization?

Capitalization is an important part of English language usage. Words are capitalized to bestow distinction, emphasis or importance. In the business world, writers often follow an in-house style guide, the latest version of *The Gregg Reference Manual* or *The Associated Press Stylebook* to capitalize acronyms, technology, social media and other specialized terms. Although not exhaustive, the following charts provide a snapshot of the most essential capitalization rules for academic and business writing.

Essential Capitalization Rules

Rule #1: Capitalize the first word of a sentence, question, or direct quotation.

> **Example:**
> - **T**risha already copied the minutes.

Rule #2: Capitalize the first word of each item in a list, bulleted list or outline.

Example:

Please order the following supplies:

- **C**opy paper
- **E**nvelopes
- **B**inder clips

Rule #3: Capitalize proper names of people, places and things.

Examples:

- **M**ela Daniels
- **T**he **B**roadway **B**ridge
- **R**iverfest

Rule #4: Capitalize languages, religions, races, and peoples.

Examples:

- **E**nglish
- **C**hristianity
- **A**frican **A**merican

Rule #5: Capitalize descriptive names or nicknames.

Examples:

- **F**irst **L**ady
- **M**eemaw
- **S**cooter

Rule #6: Capitalize words derived from proper names.

Examples:

- **C**alifornian
- **B**ostonian
- **A**rkansan

Rule #7: Capitalize academic degrees that follow a personal name whether abbreviated or written in full.

Examples:
- John Edward, **Ph.D.**
- Tina Wells, **Master of Social Sciences**

Rule #8: Capitalize college or educational course titles.

Examples:
- History 101
- Composition II
- Business Grammar Essentials

Rule #9: Capitalize days of the week.

Examples:
- Monday, Tuesday, Wednesday

Rule #10: Capitalize months of the year.

Examples:
- April, May, June

Rule #11: Capitalize holidays, holy days and seasons.

Examples:
- Christmas, Kwanzaa, Rosh Hashanah

Rule #12: Capitalize historical periods and events.

Examples:
- Reconstruction, Harlem Renaissance, World War II

Rule #13: Capitalize special events.

Examples:
- Macy's Thanksgiving Day Parade, Super Bowl LI

Rule #14: Capitalize official documents.

Examples:
- Bill of Rights, U.S. Constitution, Emancipation Proclamation

Rule #15: Capitalize formal epithets or descriptive titles.

Examples:
- Alexander the Great, Catherine the Great, The Godfather of Soul

Rule #16: Capitalize planets and heavenly bodies.

Examples:
- Mars, Earth, Venus, the Milky Way

Rule #17: Capitalize continents of the world.

Examples:
- Asia, Africa, South America, North America, Antarctica, Australia, Europe

Rule #18: Capitalize streets, roads, highways.

Examples:
- Baltimore Dr., Hinson Rd., I-630 West, U.S. Highway 101

Rule #19: Capitalize states and cities.

Examples:
- Arkansas, Texas, Little Rock, Dallas

Rule #20: Capitalize sections of a country or continent.

Examples:
- the Dirty South, the Midwest, the Middle East, the West Coast

Rule #21: Capitalize landforms.

    Examples:
- Grand Canyon, Rocky Mountains, San Andreas Fault

Rule #22: Capitalize bodies of water.

    Examples:
- Arabian Sea, Pacific Ocean, Arkansas River

Rule #23: Capitalize national parks, monuments and public areas.

    Examples:
- Central Park, Hot Springs National Park, Mount Rushmore

Rule #24: Capitalize buildings, organizations, and institutions.

    Examples:
- Marriott Hotel, Schomburg Center for Research in Black Culture

Rule #25: Capitalize family relationships when used as proper names or spiritual titles.

    Examples:
- Mother Teresa, Father Tom, Aunt Tootsie, Uncle Fish

Rule #26: Capitalize high school graduating classes.

    Examples:
- Class of '89, the Freshman Class of 2018

Rule #27: Capitalize official titles of honor and respect when they precede personal names. Civil titles follow the same rules.

    Examples:
- **Ms.** Coretta Scott King   **President** Bill Clinton
- **Reverend** Jerry D. Black   **Councilman** Terry Jones

Rule #28: Capitalize official titles when used to directly address an individual instead of their full names.

Examples:

- **Madame Secretary**, please guide us on this issue.
- **General**, the troops are in good spirits.
- **Your Honor,** I apologize.

Rule #29: Capitalize official government titles when used to address an individual or to highlight their position.

Examples:

- the **President** of the United States
- the **Queen** of England
- **Secretary** of Defense

Rule #30: Capitalize academic and religious titles when they precede or come before the person's name. Spell out **Reverend** and **Doctor** in **formal** situations.

Examples:

- **Professor** Ashan R. Hampton
- **Bishop** Silas Johnson
- **Reverend** C.L. Harvey
- **Doctor** Lia Steele

Rule #31: Capitalize academic degrees and professional designations. Write **multiple degrees** in order of importance or in the order they were earned. Your choice depends on style and intention for ranking degrees.

Examples:

- Laura Bell, **Ph.D.**
- James Palmer, **M.D.**
- Aldous Mitchell, **Ed.D, M.A.**
- Katrina Moore, **B.A., M.S.**

Rule #32: Capitalize all words in the **title of a book**, **magazine**, **movie title**, **short story**, **poem** or other **creative work**, especially the first and the last word.

However, **do not capitalize** the following **articles**, **conjunctions** and **prepositions** within the title. (See *Chapter 17 Prepositions*):

- a, an, the, and, as, but, if, or, nor, at, by, for, in, of, off
- on, out, to, up, with, within, to

Only capitalize articles, conjunctions and prepositions if the title begins with any of these short words:

- **On** the Pulse of Morning
- **The** Invisible Man
- **The** Lottery
- **A** Dream within a Dream

Rule #33: Capitalize the word **"city"** only when it is part of the corporate name of a city or part of a nickname.

Examples:
- New York **City**
- The Windy **City**
- The **city** of New Orleans

Rule #34: Capitalize the word **"state"** only when it follows the proper name of a state or is part of a nickname.

Examples:
- The **state** of Arkansas is known as the **Natural State**.

Rule #35: Capitalize the words: **North**, **South**, **East**, and **West** when they indicate specific regions or proper names.

Examples:

- in the **North**
- back **East**
- the Deep **South**
- the **West** Coast

Rule #36: Capitalize the seasons of the year when they are included in proper nouns. **Otherwise, lowercase the seasons of the year**—fall, winter, spring, and summer—when not used in a formal title.

Examples:

- Old Man **Winter**
- Dog Days of **Summer**
- fall semester
- winter catalog
- spring conference

> not titles

Rule #37: Capitalize the trade names of manufactured products. **Lowercase** the words following the trade name that are not part of the product.

Examples:

- Liquid-Plumr
- Oreo Double Stuff
- Mountain Dew
- Ivory **soap**
- Sony **television**
- Dell **computer**

Rule #38: Capitalize specific names of races, ethnicities, cultures and nationalities. Lowercase general descriptive words like "black" or "white" in reference to skin color or race.

Examples:

- African American
- Caucasian
- Chinese food
- Puerto Rican Day Parade
- black people
- white woman

> General Descriptive words

Rule #39: Capitalize the word **"committee"** only when part of a proper noun or formal name. Use lowercase when referring to general committees.

Examples:
- The House **Committee** on Education and the Workforce (formal)
- an Education and Workforce **committee** (general)

Rule #40: Capitalize the word **"subcommittee"** only when part of a proper noun or formal name. Use lowercase when referring to general subcommittees.

Examples:
- the Senate Permanent **Subcommittee** on Investigations ←*formal Name*
- the Investigations **subcommittee** ← *part of proper Noun*

Rule #41: Capitalize **"board"** and **"trustee"** only when part of a proper noun or formal name. Otherwise, use lower case.

Examples:
- Cornerstone Communications **Board** of Directors *formal Name*
- the bank's **board** of directors
- Philander Smith College **Board** of Trustees *Formal Name*

Rule #42: Capitalize job titles when they precede or come before a person's name. However, always capitalize job titles in signature lines of emails, even if the title comes after the person's name.

Examples:
- **Director of Customer Service**, Ashley Matthews
- Mark Dylan, **Operations Manager**   *Signature lines*

Lowercase job titles when they come after a person's name or when set off by commas within a sentence.

Examples:
- Dana Jones, **the editorial director** for *Essence Magazine*, stopped writing her column earlier this year.
- Mark Dylan, **operations manager**, hosts a nightly radio show.

Rule #43: Capitalize department and organizational terms when they are actual names of units within a company being referred to in internal documents. **Do not capitalize** these terms when referring to **other** company's organizations. Some common terms are marketing department, board of directors, finance committee, manufacturing division, promotions, etc.

Examples:

- The **Marketing Department** will discuss website advertising.

- Adler's **marketing department** will voice our commercials.

- Our **Board of Directors** will meet at 10 a.m.

- ACE's **board of directors** must review our proposal first.

- **Urban Promotions** landed a lucrative in-store deal.

- The ****promotions** team reviewed the contract yesterday.

---

*Note: Do not make "promotions" possessive when shortening the proper name of a department or unit. For example, "the promotions team" refers back to the full department name, "Urban Promotions."

Rule #44: Capitalize the article **"the"** only if part of the full proper name of a company or product. Otherwise, lowercase "the" when it precedes company, department or product names.

Examples:

- **The** Associated Press
- **The** Wall Street Journal
- **The** Sharper Image

Rule #45: Capitalize computer, technology, and media terms according to the style guide of your choice. However, the capitalized terms below are generally accepted across the board in business, newspaper, and web content writing.

B2B	Business-to-Business
B2C	Business-to-Consumer
B2G	Business-to-Government
CAPTCHA	Completely Automated Public Turing Test to Tell Computers and Humans Apart
CD-R	Compact Disc–Recordable
CD-ROM	Compact Disc Read-Only Memory
CD-RW	Compact Disc–Rewritable
DNS	Domain Name System
DVD	Digital Versatile Disc
DVD-R	Digital Video Disc-Recordable
DVD-RW	Digital Video Disc-Rewritable
DVR	Digital Video Recorder
FTP	File Transfer Protocol
GIF or .gif	Graphics Interface Format
HTTP	Hypertext Transfer Protocol
iPad (IPAD)	Capitalize the "i" when starting a sentence or headline.
iPhone (IPHONE)	Capitalize the "i" when starting a sentence or headline.
iPod (IPOD)	Capitalize the "i" when starting a sentence or headline.
JPEG or .jpg	Joint Photographics Experts Group
MB	Megabyte
Mbps	Megabits Per Second
MHz	Megahertz
MP3	MPEG-1 AUDIO LAYER 3
MPEG-4 or MP4	Motion Picture Experts Group
P2P	Peer to Peer Network
PDF	Portable Document Format

PNG or.png	Portable Network Graphics
POD	Publishing On Demand
	Print On Demand
RAM	Random-Access Memory
VM	Voice Mail
VoIP	Voice Over Internet Protocol
Wi-Fi	Wireless Fidelity
World Wide Web	(Spelled Out)
WWW	World Wide Web (Acronym)
XML	Extensible Markup Language

Rule #46: In general, lowercase these web-related terms, according to current practices. However, check your style guide.

Examples:

- internet
- web address
- webcast
- webmaster
- website
- web
- web browser
- webfeed
- webpage
- webcam

Capitalization Exercise

Directions: Which sentence is capitalized correctly? Write "C" for correct in the blank.

1. __I__ My Grandmother lives on Confederate boulevard. ✓

   __C__ My grandmother lives on Confederate Boulevard.

2. __I__ Erin must take a Psychology class in Spring quarter, but she
   really wants to take World History 200.

   __C__ Erin must take a psychology class in spring quarter, but she ✓
   really wants to take World History 200.

3. __I__ I am not guilty, your honor. ✓

   __C__ I am not guilty, Your Honor.

4. __I__ Uncle Mack said, "Please say left or right, not North,
   South, East or West." ✓

   __C__ Uncle Mack said, "Please say left or right, not north, south,
   east or west."

5. __I__ Coach Eddie Bland led the patriots to their first winning
   Football season. ✓

   __C__ Coach Eddie Bland led The Patriots to their first winning
   football season.

6. __C__ Senator Grant Jones addressed The Toastmaster's group.

   __I__ Grant Jones, senator, addressed the toastmaster's group. ✓

7. __C__ Carey put her iPod, dvd and MP3 player on the table.

   __I__ Carey put her iPod, DVD and MP3 player on the table. ✗

Answers: Capitalization Exercise

1. _____My Grandmother lives on Confederate boulevard.

   _____**My grandmother lives on Confederate Boulevard.**

2. _____Erin must take a Psychology class in Spring quarter, but
   she really wants to take World History 200.

   _____**Erin must take a psychology class in spring quarter, but she
   really wants to take World History 200.**

3. _____I am not guilty, your honor.

   _____**I am not guilty, Your Honor.**

4. _____Uncle Mack said, "Please say left or right, not North,
   South, East or West."

   _____**Uncle Mack said, "Please say left or right, not north, south, east
   or west."**

5. _____Coach Eddie Bland led the patriots to their first winning
   Football season.

   _____**Coach Eddie Bland led The Patriots to their first winning
   football season.**

6. _____**Senator Grant Jones addressed The Toastmaster's group.**

   _____Grant Jones, senator, addressed the toastmaster's group.

7. _____Carey put her iPod, dvd and MP3 player on the table.

   _____**Carey put her iPod, DVD and MP3 player on the table.**

Chapter Seven
Homonyms/Homophones

Photo Credit: Thinkstock Photos, Jack Hollingsworth.

Spelling Rules

American spelling rules are not the easiest to learn and pose difficulties for native English speakers and second language learners alike, because there seems to be an exception for every rule. However, correct spelling is essential to good writing, especially in business and academic settings. Misspellings suggest carelessness or a lack of intelligence. In either case, students, teachers, parents, and business professionals must take time to review and practice good spelling habits.

What is a Homonym?

Homonyms are words that share the same spelling, and the same (or similar) pronunciation, but different meanings. Homonyms are also called *look-a-likes*.

Homonyms:

- **Same** spelling

- **Same** pronunciation

- **Different** meanings

Examples:

Scale the fish.

- **Verb:** to scale

Weigh the fish on the scale.

- **Noun:** a scale

Explanation: In the example above, the words "scale" and "scale" share the same spelling, and the same pronunciation, but different meanings, which make them homonyms.

More Examples of Homonyms:

tip	*(n.)* pointed or slender end	*(v.)* giving money
suit	*(n.)* set of clothing	*(v.)* to satisfy
sole	*(n.)* bottom of a shoe	*(adj.)* the only one

What is a Homophone?

Homophones are words that share the same pronunciation, different spellings, and different meanings. Homophones are also called *sound-a-likes*.

- **Same** pronunciation

- **Different** spelling

- **Different** meanings

Homophone Examples:

Lola's **son** is handsome.

- **Noun:** a male child

The **sun** blinded my eyes.

- **Noun:** a hot, heavenly star

Explanation: In the example above, the words "son" and "sun" share the same pronunciation, but different spellings, and different meanings, which make them homophones.

More Examples of Homophones:

scent	*(n.)* a smell	**cent**	*(n.)* one penny
too	*(adv.)* excessive	**two**	*(n.)* a numeral
profit	*(n.)* extra money	**prophet**	*(n.)* a divinely inspired teacher

What is a Homograph?

Homographs are words that share the same spelling, but different pronunciation, and different meanings.

- **Same** spelling
- **Different** pronunciation
- **Different** meanings

Examples:

Dove
- **Noun:** a bird

Dove
- **Verb:** to move downward

Explanation: In the example above, the words "dove" and "dove" share the same spelling, but different pronunciation and different meanings, which make them homographs. A bird, "dove" is pronounced with the "uh" sound. The verb, "dove" is pronounced with the long "oh" sound.

More Examples of Homographs:

bow   *(n.)* a decoration   **bow**   *(v.)* to bend

record   *(n.)* a musical disc   **record**   *(v.)* to write down

escort   *(n.)* a companion   **escort**   *(v.)* to attend

Spelling Tips

1. Study common spelling rules.

2. Study lists of commonly misspelled words and practice spelling them correctly.

3. Use a dictionary or thesaurus to check for correct spellings.

4. Read a variety of materials and study correctly spelled words.

5. Become a good speller! Study. Read. Write every day. Practice makes perfect.

6. Pay close attention to words with five or more letters.

7. Pronounce words slowly to notice every syllable.

8. To improve accuracy, read aloud or touch each word when proofreading.

9. To catch spelling errors, read the page from right to left or from top to bottom.

10. Use spellchecker software...with caution! Know the rules. Correct your own spelling.

For more resources on American spelling rules, take the online class, **"Spelling Rules Refresher"** at **www.arhampton.com**. Click "Classes" to enroll.

Spelling Exercise

Directions: Circle the correct word.

1. When writing a research paper, **(cite, site)** your sources.

2. Thomas **(ate, eight)** too much food.

3. A bird **(flu, flew)** into the grocery store and scared several customers.

4. Dennis did not **(know, no)** the answer to the question the professor asked.

5. Tamika learned her multiplication tables by **(rote, wrote).**

6. My parents gave us **(they're, their)** old furniture.

7. Kevin waited **(too, two)** whole hours for his date to get dressed.

Answers: Spelling Exercise

1. cite

2. ate

3. flew

4. know

5. rote

6. their

7. two

Chapter Eight
Common Usage Errors

Photo Credit: Thinkstock Photos, BananaStock.

Who or Whoever?

Use **who** or **whoever** if you can substitute the following pronouns for the "who" phrase: **he, she, they, I, we**. These nominative pronouns function as subjects. The substitution test takes a statement and turns it into a question (or vice versa) to determine the correct usage.

Examples:

> Who is waiting?
> - **He / She** is waiting.

> Who did they say was chosen?
> - **He / She / I** was chosen.

Examples:

> The job goes to **whoever** answers the ad first.

> Who answers the ad first?
> - **He / She** answers the ad first.

Whom or Whomever?

Use **whom** or **whomever** if you can substitute the following pronouns: **him, her, them, me, us**. These pronouns function as objects of verbs or prepositions.

Examples:

> Whom did you ask to pick up the order?
> - I asked **him/ her/ them** to pick up the order.

> To whom is the mailing addressed?
> - The mailing is addressed to **him/ her/ them/ me/ us**.

I / Me or Myself?

Many people get confused on how to use personal pronouns to refer to themselves as an individual or as part of a group. As a result, otherwise smart professionals trip over these pronouns in written and verbal communication by using *"myself"* as a cover for their uncertainty.

However, there are times when inserting the personal pronouns "I" or "me" in sentences is correct, even if it sounds odd to do so. Remember, correct grammar and usage are not determined by the way words *sound* in certain combinations. Proofreaders and content creators bear the responsibility of knowing how to correctly and effectively use these pronouns.

When to use "I"

"I" is a nominative (naming) pronoun that is used as the subject of a sentence.

Example:

- **I** suggest we schedule the presentation for next Tuesday.

When to use "Me"

Use **"Me"** as the object of a verb or the object of a preposition.

Example:

- The report was distributed to Lauren and **me**.

Substitution Test:

- The report was distributed to **me**.

In the above example, you would not state, "The report was distributed to *I*. Therefore, "me" is correct in this sentence.

Between you and me

"Between you and me" is a type of idiomatic phrase that is stated the same way every time it is communicated, without variations. However, the reason "I" is incorrect in this phrase—(i.e., "between you and I")—is because objective case pronouns ("me") are used as objects of prepositions ("between"), not subjects ("I").

When to use "Myself"

As a general rule of thumb, avoid writing "myself." Only use "myself" for emphasis, reflexively, or to show that you completed an action for yourself.

Examples:

- I signed up for the conference **myself**.

- I, **myself**, used that wrinkle cream and it worked.

Common Mistakes Using "Myself"

Example #1:

- Debra and **myself** worked on the budget.

Correction:

- Debra and **I** worked on the budget.

Substitution:

- **I** worked on the budget.

Example #2:

- Mark is attending the meeting with Dawn and **myself**.

Correction:

- Mark is attending the meeting with Dawn and **me**.

Substitution:

- Mark is attending the meeting with **me**.

Affect or Effect?

Affect *(v.)*

- to influence; to change; to assume

Examples:

- The reorganization will **affect** the radio broadcast staff.
- Financial problems often **affect** career decisions.

Effect *(n.)*

- an outcome or result

Effect *(v.)*

- to cause to happen; to bring about

Examples:

- Weight gain is an **effect** of high stress. **(Noun)**
- High stress **effects** weight gain. **(Verb)**

Lay or Lie?

Lay *(v.)*

- to put or place something; usually refers to inanimate objects.

Example #1:

- When you finish with the reports, please **lay** them on my desk.

Lie *(v.)*

- to rest or recline; usually refers to people or living beings.

Example #2:

- All she wanted was to **lie** down on the couch after a long day of classes.

See / Saw or Seen?

The word "see" is an irregular verb that changes spellings to form the past tense, such as "saw." When forming a past participle phrase, "seen" is used along with the helping verbs *has*, *have* or *had*. Unfortunately, many English speakers commonly misuse this verb, as in the examples below.

Example #1:

- She looked as if she **seen** a ghost.

Correction #1:

- She looked as if she **had seen** a ghost.

Example #2:

- I **seen** her coming out of the grocery store yesterday.

Correction #2:

- I **saw** her coming out of the grocery store yesterday.

Sit or Set?

Sit *(v.)*

- to assume an upright position

Example #1:

- Uncle Dutch **sits** in his favorite chair like a stately king.

Set *(v.)*

- to put or place something

Example #2:

- Ask the accountants to **set** their materials in the next office.

Looking for an extra challenge?

Proofreading Power: Skills & Drills provides essential rules, guidelines and tips to quickly boost your editing prowess.

Ordering information:

www.arhampton.com

Correcting Confusing Pairs

a *(article)*	precedes nouns that start with a consonant letter or consonant sound
an *(article)*	precedes nouns that start with a vowel letter or vowel sound
accept *(v.)*	to receive or take
except *(prep.)*	excluding or omitting
advice *(n.)*	a recommendation or opinion
advise *(v.)*	to counsel
a lot *(adv.)*	a large quantity; great extent
alot *(adv.)*	incorrect spelling; write as two separate words
allot *(v.)*	to divide or distribute; parcel out
all ready *(adj.)*	all prepared
already *(adv.)*	previously; by or before this time
all right *(adv.)*	satisfactory; acceptable
alright *(adv.)*	incorrect spelling; write as two separate words
all-right *(adj.)*	agreeable, acceptable or commendable
all together *(adv.)*	in a group
altogether *(adv.)*	wholly, entirely; completely
alumnus/alumni *(n.)*	graduates; former members of an organization
alumna/alumnae *(n.)*	a female graduate or former female student
assure *(v.)*	to make confident
ensure *(v.)*	to make certain something happens
insure *(v.)*	to issue or purchase insurance
awhile *(adv.)*	for a short period of time
a while *(n.)*	a noun phrase describing a period of time
among *(prep.)*	used for more than two persons or things
between *(prep.)*	used with two persons or things
beside *(prep.)*	next to; near; at the side of
besides *(adv.)*	in addition to; furthermore
biannual *(adj.)*	occurring twice a year
biennial *(adj.)*	occurring every two years
semiannual *(adj.)*	occurring every six months or twice a year
biweekly *(adj.)*	occurring every two weeks; (26 paychecks)

bimonthly *(adj.)*	occurring twice a month; (24 paychecks)
bimonthly *(adj.)*	occurring every two months; (6 paychecks)
bring *(v.)*	motion toward the speaker
take *(v.)*	motion away from the speaker
can (could) *(v.)*	ability, power or skill
may (might) *(aux.v.)*	permission, possibility or probability
capital *(n.)*	location of government in a city, state or country
capitol *(n.)*	a government building
cite *(v.)*	to quote or state
sight *(n.)*	scene or view
site *(n.)*	location
complement *(n.)*	something that completes
complement *(v.)*	to complete or make perfect
compliment *(n.)*	a flattering remark
compliment *(v.)*	to praise
compose *(v.)*	to create, form, write, produce; to put together
composed (of) *(v.)*	to make up or form the basis of
comprise *(v.)*	to include, contain or consist of
continual *(adj.)*	occurring at frequent intervals
continuous *(adj.)*	occurring without pauses or interruptions
convince *(v.)*	to change a person's mind by argument
persuade *(v.)*	to win over, influence or move to action
criteria *(n.)*	standards of judgment or criticism
criterion *(n.)*	the singular form of "criteria"
disinterested *(adj.)*	impartial; showing no preferences or prejudice
uninterested *(adj.)*	bored or lacking interest
eager *(adj.)*	fervent, enthusiastic
anxious *(adj.)*	full of anxiety or worry due to apprehension
each other *(pron.)*	describing reciprocity between two nouns
one another *(pron.)*	reciprocity between three or more nouns
everyday *(adj.)*	ordinary, commonplace; daily occurrence
every day *(adj.)*	each day

emigrate *(v.)*	leaving one country or region to settle in another country
immigrate *(v.)*	coming to a country as a foreigner to live
farther *(adv.)*	refers to physical distance
further *(adv.)*	refers to degree or extent
fewer *(adj.)*	a smaller number than expected; used with plural nouns
fewer *(n.)*	a small number (of something); single items
less *(adj.)*	a lower extent, amount, or degree; quantities
i.e. *(abbr.)*	Latin *id est;* (that is)
e.g. *(abbr.)*	Latin *exempli gratia;* (for example)
imply *(v.)*	to suggest
infer *(v.)*	to deduce from evidence
its *(adj.)*	possessive form of "it"
it's *(contr.)*	contraction of "it is" or "it has"
lets *(v.)*	to allow or permit; singular of the verb "let"
let's *(contr.)*	the contraction of "let us"
nauseous *(adj.)*	affected with a feeling of sickness or disgust
nauseate *(v.)*	causing stomach upset, disgust or loathing
principal *(n.)*	first or highest in rank; chief official of a school
principle *(n.)*	a general truth; a rule; integrity
pseudo *(adj.)*	false, pretending or unauthentic
quasi *(adj.)*	so-called; resembling or seeming, but not really
stationary *(adj.)*	fixed in one position
stationery *(n.)*	paper for writing
than *(conj.)*	used after a comparison
then *(adv.)*	next; in that case
their *(adj.)*	belonging to them; possessive form of they
there *(adv.)*	in that place
they're *(contr.)*	contraction of *they are*
well *(adj.)*	in good health; satisfactory, pleasing or proper
good *(adj.)*	suitable, competent, pleasant; well-founded

whereas *(conj.)*	on the contrary; in view of the fact that; since
whereby *(conj.)*	by which; according to which; the means of
wherein *(adv.)*	in what way; in what respect
year's experience *(adj.)*	one singular year of experience
years' experience *(adj.)*	more than one year of experience

Usage Exercise

Directions: Circle the appropriate word.

1. There is a conflict **(among, between)** operations and marketing.

2. The reorganization will **(affect, effect)** the home office as well as the regional offices.

3. When you are finished with the reports, please **(lay, lie)** them on my desk.

4. The Sales Department has set its goals **(farther, further)** than the Marketing Department.

5. We are **(all ready, already)** to begin work on the Fullerton project.

6. Be sure to submit all travel expenses to either Kate or **(I, me).**

7. I will speak to **(whoever, whomever)** answers the telephone.

Answers: Usage Exercise

1. between

2. affect

3. lay

4. further

5. all ready

6. me

7. whomever

Chapter Nine
Active/Passive Voice

Photo Credit: Thinkstock Photos, Stockbyte.

What is Active Voice?

In **active voice**, the subject is the doer of the action. The subject of the sentence directly performs the action. The active voice uses the simple or root form of the verb.

Example #1:

- Our technical **editors** frequently **update** the instruction manuals.

    subject = editors   **verb** = update

Explanation: In this example, the editors directly perform the action of updating the manuals. Therefore, the sentence is written in active voice.

Example #2:

- Claire's **team** **cut** the budget twenty-five percent.

In the above example, **team** is the simple subject, and **Claire's team** is the full subject. The verb is **cut,** which is not preceded by auxiliary or helping verbs, and is therefore in its root form.

Explanation: Since it is clear that Claire's team performed the action of cutting the budget, this sentence is written in **active voice**. Also note that **the budget** is the **direct object**, because it receives the action of the verb; it is the thing being cut.

What is Passive Voice?

In **passive voice**, the performer follows the verb and appears to receive the action of the verb. Also, a form of the verb "to be" precedes the main verb. Sometimes the passive voice defines or describes something without direct activity from a performer.

Example #3:

- The **budget** **was cut** twenty-five percent by Claire's team.

    subject = budget   **verb** = was cut

Explanation: In passive voice, the parts of the sentence seem reversed, but the subject, verb and direct object still hold the same functions as in active voice. The **budget** is now in the subject slot, and the performer, **Claire's team**, appears to assume the direct object's position.

Therefore, the **passive voice** makes the performer of the action unclear, because the performer is usually the subject. A budget is not a person, and cannot cut twenty-five percent, but the people on Claire's team can cut a budget.

- **Who cut the budget?** = Claire's team

- **What was cut?** = the budget

- **What action is being performed?** = cut / was cut (the budget)

Compare the **active** and **passive** versions of this sentence to further understand the differences:

Active Voice:

- Claire's **team cut** the budget twenty-five percent.

Passive Voice:

- The **budget was cut** twenty-five percent by Claire's team.

The active voice is preferable, because it is clear and concise. Take a look at a few more examples of sentences written in the active and passive voice:

Active: Our **technical editors** frequently **update** the instruction manuals.

Passive: The **instruction manuals are frequently** updated by our technical editors.

Active: **Sherri ate** a candy bar.

Passive: A **candy bar was eaten** by Sherri.

Active: The **teacher lost** my child's final exam.

Passive: My child's **final exam was lost** by the teacher.

Reminders:

- In active voice, the subject of the sentence directly performs the action.

- **Active verbs <u>do not</u>** include forms of **"to be"** or helping/auxiliary verbs (i.e. has, have, had, is, be, being).

- **Passive verbs** include forms of **"to be"** preceding the root verb.

- In **passive voice**, the true performer of the action sometimes follows the verb.

- The **passive** voice can also **define** or **describe** something without direct activity from a performer.

Learn more about the **active/passive voice,** and other advanced grammar topics in the online class, **"Business Grammar Bootcamp"** at **www.arhampton.com**. Click "Classes" to enroll.

Active/Passive Voice Exercise

Directions: Indicate whether the following sentences are **active** or **passive**.

1. _____ Jeff took twenty-four pictures of his new sports car.

2. _____The music industry's platinum records are usually made of nickel and are covered with foil or paint, not platinum.

3. _____The gingko tree dates back to the time of the dinosaurs.

4. _____The performance reports were signed by the team leader.

5. _____The slash mark used in fractions is known as a virgule.

6. _____ A group of lions is called a pride, and a flock of larks is an exaltation.

7. _____Two inmates escaped from jail during an altercation.

Answers: Active/Passive Exercise

1. active

2. passive

3. active

4. passive

5. passive

6. passive

7. active

Chapter Ten
Shifts in Verb Tense

Photo Credit: Thinkstock Photos, Ciaran Griffin.

What are Shifts in Verb Tense?

Shifts in verb tense occur when one of the verbs in a sentence is out of format with the rest. Basically, all the verbs in the sentence are not parallel or not written in the same verb tense.

- Remember, **verb tenses** indicate time: **past, present or future**.

Example:

- My Irish Setter, Pancake, **sits** in the front seat of the car and **barked** at a passing cyclist.

Explanation: The verbs are ***sits*** and ***barked***. "Sits" is a present tense verb. "Barked" is a past tense verb. This is confusing to the reader, and represents a shift in tense.

Is the action happening **now** or did it happen a while ago in the **past**?

In order to clarify the timeline, both **verbs** must be in the **same tense**. To correct the sentence, make both of the verbs **present tense** or both of the verbs **past tense**.

Correcting Shifts in Verb Tense

Original Sentence:

- My Irish Setter, Pancake, **sits** in the front seat of the car and **barked** at a passing cyclist.

Correction #1 (Past Tense):

- My Irish Setter, Pancake, **sat** in the front seat of the car and **barked** at a passing cyclist.

Correction #2 (Present Tense):

- My Irish Setter, Pancake, **sits** in the front seat of the car and **barks** at a passing cyclist.

Consider this:

If someone were telling about this dog in **real-time**, wouldn't the **present progressive tense** sound and feel a bit better?

Alternate Phrasing (Present Progressive Tense):

- My Irish Setter, Pancake, **is sitting** in the front seat of the car and **barking** at a passing cyclist.

In present progressive tense, the action is happening right now, real-time, as you speak.

More Corrections:

Example #3:

- Dana **watched** the horse that **grazes** in the lower meadow.

Correction:

- Dana **watched** the horse that **grazed** in the lower meadow.

Remember: If **more than one verb** appears in a sentence, use the **first verb** to determine the tense for all the other verbs.

Example #4:

- When the game **ended**, the fans **rush** onto the field.

Correction:

- When the game **ended**, the fans **rushed** onto the field.

Example #5:

- Rosita **keeps** the best items for her own collection and **sold** the rest.

Correction:

- Rosita **keeps** the best items for her own collection and **sells** the rest.

Reminders:

- **Shifts in tense** occur when one of the **verbs** in a sentence is out of format with the rest.

- In order to clarify the timeline, **both verbs** must be in the **same tense**.

- If **more than one verb** appears in the sentence, use the **first verb** to determine the tense for all the other verbs. However, use the verb tense that makes the most sense for your writing project.

Knowledge Check

Directions: Write your answer in the space provided or circle the correct answer.

1. When do shifts in verb tense occur?

2. Verb tenses indicate_____.

3. Passive voice includes a form of the verb_____.

4. In_____the subject is the doer of the action.

5. High stress **(affects / effects)** your medical health.

6. Please **(lay / lie)** your yoga mat on the floor.

7. Only use the pronoun "myself" for_____.

Shifts in Verb Tense Exercise

Directions: Identify the sentence **with a shift in verb tense**. Circle the appropriate letter.

1.

a. Advisors will tell their students to register early so that they got the classes they wanted.

b. Advisors will tell their students to register early so that they get the classes they want.

2.

a. In 1835, Charles Darwin explored the Galapagos Islands, and in 1850 he writes *Origin of Species.*

b. In 1835, Charles Darwin explored the Galapagos Islands, and in 1850 he wrote *Origin of Species.*

3.

a. In the interview, the star of the film explained the stunt work and talked about the special effects. However, she never mentions her costars.

b. In the interview, the star of the film explained the stunt work and talked about the special effects. However, she never mentioned her costars.

4.

a. The virus mutated so rapidly that it developed a resistance to most vaccines.

b. The virus mutated so rapidly that it develops a resistance to most vaccines.

5.

a. I am giving my sister a Barbie doll and bought her a birthday cake.

b. I gave my sister a Barbie doll and bought her a birthday cake.

6.

    a. I started writing my thesis four weeks ago, but I was finishing it right before class despite my early preparation.

    b. I started writing my thesis four weeks ago, but I finished it right before class despite my early preparation.

7.

    a. By the time Chad is finished cramming for finals, he studied for seven hours.

    b. By the time Chad is finished cramming for finals, he will have studied for seven hours.

Answers on back of page.

Answers: Shifts in Verb Tense Exercise

1. a

2. a

3. a

4. b

5. a

6. a

7. a

Chapter Eleven
Shifts in Person & Voice

Photo Credit: Unsplash.com, Jonathan Francisca.

What is Person?

Person refers to the pronouns used to refer to people or things within a sentence. Person also distinguishes the speaker (first person) from the person or people being spoken to (second person), and those being spoken about (third person).

First Person Pronouns:

- I, me, my, mine, we, us, our

Second Person Pronouns:

- you, your, yours

Third Person Pronouns:

- he, his, him, she, her, hers, it, its, one, they, them, their

What is a Shift in Person?

A **shift in person** occurs when a writer jumps from first to second or third person in one sentence or in one longer piece of writing. Basically, the pronoun references are not consistent.

Example #1:

- If **one** wants an application, **they** should ask the principal.

Correction:

- If **they** want an application, **they** should ask the principal.

Example #2:

- When **you** see an opportunity, **he** should take advantage of it.

Correction:

- When **you** see an opportunity, **you** should take advantage of it.

Example #3:

- If **they** speak Spanish, **we** should be able to understand Italian.

Correction:

- If **they** speak Spanish, **they** should be able to understand Italian.

What is a Shift in Voice?

A **shift in voice** occurs when the verbs jump from active to passive in one sentence or in one longer piece of writing. Voice refers to whether or not the verbs are active or passive.

Example #1:

- As the joggers rounded a curve, a beautiful lake was seen near the hills.

Explanation: The first half of the sentence includes an **active verb** where the performers—(joggers)—take an action—round a curve. However, the second half of the sentence is written in **passive voice** where "a beautiful lake was seen." Who saw the lake? The performer is unclear.

Original Sentence:

- As the joggers rounded a curve, a beautiful lake was seen near the hills.

Correction (Active):

- As the joggers rounded a curve, **they saw** a beautiful lake near the hills.

Consider this revision (Active):

- The joggers rounded a curve and saw a beautiful lake near the hills.

Example #2:

- Although Miranda tried to get to Zumba on time, the first half of the class **was missed**.

Correction (Active):

- Although Miranda tried to get to Zumba on time, **she missed** the first half of the class.

Reminders:

- **Shifts in Person** refer to pronoun usage: first, second or third person.

- **Shifts in Voice** refer to active or passive verbs.

- **Shifts in Tense** refer to the verb timeline: present, past or future.

Knowledge Check

Directions: Write your answer in the space provided or circle the correct answer.

1. Error that mixes pronouns_____.

2. Error that mixes active and passive verbs_____.

3. Error that mixes time sequence_____.

4. A_____is a word or phrase that describes something.

5. Carrots **(furnish / furnishes)** vitamin A to the body.

6. Yoga and meditation **(soothes / soothe)** the soul.

7. Two complete sentences separated by a comma is a_____.

Shifts in Person & Voice Exercise

Directions: Indicate whether the sentence contains a **shift in person** or a **shift in voice** by writing **"person"** or **"voice"** in the blank.

1. _____ Jo jumped when the door slammed and the tray of dishes was dropped.

2. _____ If they want a quick refund, you should file your tax return early.

3. _____ We painted the outside of the canoe blue and the inside was painted red.

4. _____ If you polish your CDs regularly, one can keep them from skipping.

5. _____ As Angie cleaned the attic, a valuable antique bottle was found.

6. _____ If you want to be taken seriously, someone should think before they speak.

7. _____ Because Kyoto stopped to get a newspaper, her train was almost missed.

Answers: Shifts in Person & Voice Exercise

1. voice

2. person

3. voice

4. person

5. voice

6. person

7. voice

Chapter Twelve
Comma Usage

Photo Credit: Pexels, Burst.

When to Use Commas

Commas often confuse even the best writers and editors. Some are partial to commas and use them generously while others economically and reluctantly punctuate sentences with commas. The goal of this section is to provide the most common and essential comma rules that should be followed, regardless of preference. However, consult and follow a style guide, if one is required.

The Oxford Comma

Do you place a comma before the conjunction "and" or not? The Oxford comma is an optional comma before the word "and" or "or" within a series or list of three or more items. Staffers Oxford University Press traditionally punctuate list items in this way, ergo, its name. The Oxford comma is also called the "serial" comma.

According to English grammar and usage rules, **inserting the additional comma is optional.** So, dropping the comma before "and" or "or" in a series should not be marked as an error. In fact, the AP does not adopt the serial comma. Therefore, including the Oxford comma is a matter of preference, but in all circumstances, clarity is the primary goal of good writing.

Essential Comma Rules

Rule #1:	Example:
Use a comma to separate a series of three or more items: nouns, verbs or adjectives.	• Tim arrived at the airport, waited in line, checked his baggage, **and** walked down the concourse to the plane.

Rule #2:	Example (No Oxford Comma):
In a list of items, putting a **comma** before the conjunction **"and"** (or "or") is *technically* optional.	• Sheila placed the order for magazines, newspapers **and** cookbooks.
The optional comma before the word "and" within a series or list of items is called the **Oxford comma**, which is used for the sake of clarity. Either way is correct.	**Example (Oxford Comma):** • Sheila placed the order for magazines, newspapers, **and** cookbooks.

Rule #3:	Examples:
Use a **comma** after an **introductory word**, **phrase** or **dependent** clause.	• **Before you call**, send a text.
Clauses can appear at the **beginning** or **end** of a sentence.	• Shana moved to Mexico, **after leaving New York**.

Rule #4:	Example:
Use a **comma** after the **day** and **calendar year** when citing a full date that include the month, day and year.	• Ahnna will arrive on **September 9, 2018,** for the training session.

Rule #5:	**Example:**
No **comma** is necessary in a date when using the **month** and year only.	• Ahnna will arrive in **September 2018** for the training session.
Rule #6:	**Examples:**
Use **commas** to separate dates from the rest of a sentence.	• **June 25, 2009,** was a sad day for Michael Jackson fans.
	• **Thursday, June 25, 2009,** was a sad day for Michael Jackson fans.
Rule #7:	**Examples:**
Use a **comma** to separate **two** or **more adjectives** that describe a noun.	• The applicant was **professional, knowledgeable,** and **experienced** in the area of accounting.
	• Texas is a **hot, dry, southern** state.
Rule #8:	**Examples:**
When **directly addressing someone** in the body of your document, enclose the **name** in commas.	• Thank you, **Wayne,** for responding so quickly to my request.
	• The manager is counting on you, **Ms. Harris,** to process the order this week.
Rule #9:	**Examples:**
Use **commas** to enclose parenthetical words, phrases or clauses, especially appositives.	• The additional supply order, **however,** will not ship until early tomorrow.
Appositives rename or give more detail about the subject, such as in the second example, *"our chapter president."*	• Ms. Mel Temple, **our chapter president,** will speak now.

Rule #10:

Use a **comma** before **conjunctions** when joining **two complete sentences** or **two parts** of a sentence.

Examples:

- There are two job openings in the English department, **and** I know you will get one of them!

- Teresa and Kerrie would like to attend the Zumba conference, **but** cannot afford the expensive fees.

Rule #11:

Use a **comma** before the word **"not"** to express a negative thought, opinion or circumstance.

Examples:

- I want mustard, **not mayonnaise,** on my burger.

- Terence sets the security code at closing, **not Melanie**.

Rule #12:

Use a **comma** after an **adverb** that comes at the beginning of a sentence.

Examples:

- **Finally,** I can get some work done.
- **Actually,** you cannot get paid for working overtime on the weekend.

Rule #13:

Put a **comma** after the words **"Yes"** or **"No"** when they begin a sentence.

Examples:

- **Yes,** I love turkey sandwiches.
- **No,** I did not edit the annual report; Adam did.

Rule #14:

Use **commas** to separate parts of a **mailing address,** especially the **city** and **state**.

Examples:

- Send the check to 171 State St., **Dallas, Texas 89332**.
- **Little Rock, Arkansas** is a great city for families and the elderly.

Rule #15:

Use **commas** in **numbers** larger than **999**.

Examples:

- The company paid **$27,325** for computer upgrades last year.

- Give us **1,000** bottles of spring water for the race this Saturday.

Rule #16:	**Examples:**
Use **commas** after **Jr.**, **Sr.** or **Arabic numbers** only if the person prefers this format. Otherwise, do not insert a comma after these suffixes.	• Chris Darby, Jr. (preferred) • Chris Darby Jr. (current rule) • Phillip James III
Rule #17:	**Examples:**
Use **commas** after abbreviated **academic**, **professional** or **religious titles** that follow a person's name.	• Cara Daniels, **Ph.D.** • Francis DeWitt, **Esq.** • Rev. Carl Dunn, **S.J.**
Rule #18:	**Examples:**
Only use **commas** to set off abbreviations like **Inc., Ltd., LLC** or **Co.** if the company prefers this format. However, check your current style guide.	• Time, Inc. (preferred) • Time Inc. (current rule) • Cooper Industries Ltd. • Domino's Pizza LLC

Knowledge Check

Directions: Circle the correct answer.

1. **(Active / Passive)** English is studied by many people in the world.

2. **(Active / Passive)** Teresa writes children's books.

3. **(Active / Passive)** I was surprised by Greg's sudden decision to leave.

4. Angela **(write / writes)** lots of emails at work.

5. Tourists in Madrid **(is / are)** well-behaved.

6. **(Basically / Basically,)** Tam knows more than the dentist.

7. Chet donated **(2750 / 2,750)** books to the library.

Answers: 1. passive 2. active 3. passive 4. writes 5. are 6. Basically, 7. 2,750

Comma Usage Exercise

Directions: Proofread the following sentences for omitted commas. Add commas where necessary.

1. Alex put lettuce onions walnuts olives and cheese in the salad.

2. The coach a cigar-chewing bully pushed his team to first place.

3. Samuel a dedicated maintenance man won an award for outstanding service to the Bugle Box Company.

4. A letter postmarked Bismarck North Dakota came for you today.

5. It seems impossible to get tickets for *Wicked* which is one of the biggest Broadway hits in years.

6. Charles will always remember June 10 1985 as the day he became office manager bought a house and became a father.

7. The company's latest model a combination felt-tipped pen and lead pencil sells for under $5.

Answers: Comma Usage Exercise

1. Alex put lettuce, onions, walnuts, olives, and cheese in the salad.

   OR

   Alex put lettuce, onions, walnuts, olives and cheese in the salad.

2. The coach, a cigar-chewing bully, pushed his team to first place.

3. Samuel, a dedicated maintenance man, won an award for outstanding service to the Bugle Box Company.

4. A letter postmarked Bismarck, North Dakota, came for you today.

5. It seems impossible to get tickets for *Wicked*, which is one of the biggest Broadway hits in years.

6. Charles will always remember June 10, 1985, as the day he became office manager, bought a house, and became a father.

   OR

   Charles will always remember June 10, 1985, as the day he became office manager, bought a house **and** became a father.

7. The company's latest model, a combination felt-tipped pen and lead pencil, sells for under $5.

Chapter Thirteen
Punctuation

Photo Credit: Thinkstock Photos, Jupiterimages.

Punctuation Essentials

In today's digital world of text messages, abbreviations and emoticons, punctuation is often omitted from sentences. However, in addition to commas, punctuation marks are essential to comprehending messages according to the writer's original intentions. Despite arguments to the contrary, effective punctuation usage is still important to good sentence construction.

Although not an exhaustive list, this chapter covers the general guidelines for the most common punctuation scenarios encountered in academic and business writing. Proofreaders and copyeditors in professional environments might find themselves revising a range of documents that require absolute attention to detail, including punctuation. Since it is impossible for most of us to remember every single rule for each punctuation mark, consult your preferred style guide, when in doubt. In particular, *The Associated Press Stylebook* differs on several rules presented in this chapter.

Apostrophe

Singular Possession:	**Examples:**
Use an **apostrophe** to show **possession** or ownership (singular).	• **Sharon's** loft
	• **Women's** department
	• **Grant's** briefcase
Add an **apostrophe + s ('s)** to nouns not ending with the letter **"s"**.	• A **student's** desk
	• A **day's** pay

Singular Possession:	**Examples:**
Add an ***apostrophe + s ('s)*** to nouns that end with the letter **"s"—after** the final **"s"**.	• The **boss's** desk
	• The **witness's** testimony
	• **Congress's** plans
	• Ms. **Jones's** garden
	• Mr. **Stephens's** car

Plural Possession:	**Examples:**
Use an **apostrophe + s (s')** to show **possession** or plural ownership.	• The **shrubs'** leaves
	• The **investors' money**
	• A **guys'** night out
Add an **apostrophe + s (s')** to plural nouns **after** the final **"s"**.	• The **twins'** room
	• The **teachers'** lounge

Plural Proper Surnames:	**Examples:**
To show possession for **plural proper** (last) **names** that do not already end with an **"s"**, add an apostrophe after the final **"s"**.	• The **Hamptons'** dog
	• The **Darlings'** mailbox
	• The **Hodges'** farm
	• The **Jacksons'** reunion
	• The **Jeffersons'** cleaners

Apostrophes *(Cont'd)*

Plural Proper Surnames:

If the last name already ends with an **"s,"** add the suffix **es** to make it plural.

Next, add an **apostrophe** *after* the final **"es" (es')** to show plural possession.

Examples:

- **NOT:** the **Jones'** new car
- **BUT:** the **Joneses** new car

Examples:

- the **Joneses'** new car
- the **Harrises'** yard
- the **Jameses'** treehouse

Dual Possession (Joint):

When two (or more) people own something jointly, add an *apostrophe* + *s* **('s) after** the **last** person listed.

Examples:

- Mary and **Jane's** business
- Martin and **Eve's** house
- Mom and **Dad's** will
- Bob, Macy and **Pam's** restaurant

Plural Possession (Separate):

When mentioning two (or more) people with distinctive or separate possession, add an *apostrophe* + *s* **('s) after each person** listed.

Examples:

- Professor **Young's** and Professor **Wyatt's** teaching styles are different.
- **Tiffany's** and **James's** kids are very talented.

Compound Words (Singular):

For **compound** words with no final **"s"** at the end, and an *apostrophe* + *s* **('s)** to show **singular possession.**

For nouns with a final **"s"**, add an *apostrophe* + **s ('s) after** the final **"s".**

Examples:

- **stockholder's** advice
- **notary public's** seal
- **attorney general's** workload
- **eyewitness's** account
- **sunglasses's** tint

Apostrophes *(Cont'd)*

Compound Words (Plural): For plural nouns **with** a final *"s"*, add an *apostrophe* **+ s** *(s')* *after* the final *"s"*.	**Examples:** • **stockholders'** shares • **vice presidents'** meeting • **wheeler-dealers'** choices • **attorney generals'** cases • **professors'** pay raise
Special Plurals: Use an **apostrophe** to show plurals for single letters. Some style guides support omitting the apostrophe, but most add it for the sake of clarity.	**Examples:** • Dot your **i's**; cross your **t's**. • Watch your **p's** and **q's**. • straight **A's** • **yes's** and **no's** • two **Ph.D.'s**
Contractions: Use an **apostrophe** where one or more **letters** have been omitted. • **can't** (cannot) • **it's** (it is) • **isn't** (is not) • **Ol'** Yeller (old)	**Examples:** • I **can't** attend your performance tonight. • **It's** not easy to create a social media marketing plan. • **Isn't** Mary taking vacation next week?
Numbers: Use an **apostrophe** where one or more **numbers** have been omitted. ******Some style guides support omitting the apostrophe, but most add it for the sake of clarity.	**Examples:** • Class of **'89** (1989) • Summer of **'99** (1999) • the **1990's** (1990s)****** • the **80's** (80s) ******

Asterisk

Do not **leave** a space **before** or **after** the **asterisk***.	**Examples:** • ***Note:** "50% of marriages end in divorce."
Use an **asterisk** to refer readers to a **footnote** at the end of a **page** or **table**.	• ***Read** *Sacred Marriage* by Gary Thomas.
Use an **asterisk** to replace profanity or other words deemed unprintable.	• Beau got fired after calling the boss a ridiculous *******.

Bracket

Use **brackets** when inserting additional words to a verbatim quote, for clarity. Verbatim means word-for-word or exactly as spoken.	**Examples:** • After the incident, Tanya Reed said, "Please respect our family's privacy and keep your options **[opinions]** to yourself."
Use **brackets** and **[*sic*]** to indicate that a word in a direct quote or in printed material has been misspelled. Note that the current AP Stylebook eliminates the use of **[sic]**.	• I am enclosing the **monie [sic]** for the campaign fund.

Colon

- **Colons** signal to the reader that there is more to come.

- **Colons** are marks of addition or expectation.

- **Colons** introduce lists and numbers.

Colon Usage

Lists (Numbered or Bulleted):	**Examples:**
Use a **colon** to introduce lists. A **complete sentence** must **precede** or come before the listed items.	• **The following cities were represented at regionals:** Dallas, Atlanta, Memphis, and New Orleans.

Insert a **colon** before these **signal phrases** that introduce a list: *for example*, *namely*, *the following*, or *as follows*.	• **Please buy the following items from the office supply store:**
	   1. paper clips
	   2. file folders
	   3. sticky notes

Clock Time:	**Examples:**
Use a **colon** to separate **hours** and **minutes** in time related phrases.	• 7:15 a.m. • 1:30 p.m. • 11:11 p.m.
Ratios:	**Examples:**
Use a **colon** to express **ratios**.	• **4:1** ratio of single women to men • **5:1** betting odds
Business Documents:	**Examples:**
Use a **colon** after a **salutation**, **subject line**, **attention line** or **enclosure** notation in a business letter or memo. Insert **one** or **two spaces** after a **colon** to clearly separate words from this punctuation mark.	• Dear Mr. Harris: • Subject: • Attention: • Enclosure: • Under separate cover:

Colon Usage *(Cont'd)*

Publication Titles: Use a **colon** to separate a **book** or **report title** from a subtitle.	**Examples:** • *Guerilla Marketing:* Public Relations Strategies for Writers • *Urban Grammar:* What You Should Say and Why
Short Phrases: Use a **colon** to connect **complete sentences** with **short phrases**. *(Yes, at times, a semicolon works as well.)	**Examples:** • Darlene finally got what she deserved: **a pink slip**. • I haven't used a typewriter in ages; **not since high school**.
Complete Sentences: Use a **colon** to connect two **complete sentences** that are closely related. *In this scenario, using a **colon** or a **semicolon** is a style preference; either one is correct.	**Examples:** • The colon is versatile: **many usage options are available**. • Many pet owners forget this deadly warning; **dogs cannot eat chocolate**.
Long Quotes: Use a **colon** to introduce a **long quote**. *Consult a style manual for exact formatting and punctuation (e.g., APA, MLA, Chicago).	**Examples:** • **In the article, *The United States Needs a Post-Election Peace Plan*, Brian Klass writes:** "For the first time in its modern history, the United States is going to need a post-election reconciliation plan."

Diagonal/Slash

Use **diagonals** in **abbreviations** and expressions of **time**.	**Examples:** • c/o (care of) • b/s (bill of sale) • w/ (with) • 24/7
Use **slashes** to express alternatives.	**Examples:** • on/off switch • AM/FM
Use **diagonals** to express **two functions** or components.	**Examples:** • owner/manager • client/server network
Use **slashes** to write fractions. ** **Do not** leave a space before or after the slash, also called a *virgule*.	**Examples:** • 2/3 of the votes • 1/2 of the audience

Ellipsis

Use the **ellipsis** to indicate **missing words** from a quotation.	**Examples:** • "Darkness cannot drive out darkness. . ." said Dr. Martin L. King, Jr.
Use the **ellipsis** to express **thoughts** that trail off.	• "You took the money, closed the account and. . .?"
Use the **ellipsis** to express a deliberate pause or to *throw shade*.	• My art show is tonight. Bring a friend. . .if you have one. • I'll come to your *next* art show . . .if there is one.

Em Dash (Dash)

- **Em dashes** are longer than hyphens.

- **Em dashes** do not include a space before or after.

- **Em dashes** are also referred to as *dashes*.

Em dashes set off single words or phrases to show special emphasis.	**Examples:** • **Zumba**—that's what he lives for every Saturday morning. • **Power, money, fame**—these were her aspirations in life.
Em dashes set off a series.	**Example:** • **The winners—Allen, Stacey and Danny**—have entered the finals.
Em dashes indicate a sudden interruption in thought or a break in sentence structure.	**Example:** • The title—**if it has a title**—is missing from the page.
Em dashes precede the words *these*, *they* and *all* when summarizing a list of details.	**Examples:** • Radio, magazines, and newspapers—**these** will suffer major advertising losses. • Tina, Mark, and Bethany—**they** all won scholarships. • Arkansas, Texas, Louisiana—**all** are important markets for new business.

En Dash (Hyphen)

Use **hyphens** to show a range of numbers. Remember, hyphens are shorter than em dashes.	**Examples:** • 1997-2001 • 8:00 a.m.-5:00 p.m. • pp. 11-40
Use **hyphens** to indicate the life span of someone who is still alive.	**Examples:** • President Bill Clinton **(1946-)** • Beyoncé Giselle Carter **(1981-)**
Use **hyphens** to indicate a period of time that spans two back-to-back calendar years.	**Examples:** • Spring **2017-2018** • Fiscal year **2000-2001**
Hyphenate numbers from **21 to 99**.	**Examples:** • Chris bought **thirty-two** assorted bags of candy for Halloween. • Tammy owes four hundred and **ninety-six** dollars in late tax fees.
Use **hyphens** to express **compound words** or **adjectives**.	**Examples:** • **Hot-water** bottle • **Make-up** brushes • **Half-chocolate-half-vanilla**
Use **hyphens** in **telephone numbers**.	**Examples:** • 888-777-9311 • (282) 541-1908 • 1-800-FLOWERS
Use **hyphens** for **ages** acting as adjectives or nouns.	**Examples:** • **100-year-old** house • A bunch of **3-year-olds**

Exclamation Point

Use **exclamation points** to end sentences that express strong emotion.	**Examples:** • **Stop!** The light is red**!** • What a great room**!**
Use **exclamation points** instead of a question mark to express strong emotion.	**Examples:** • What did I tell you**!** • How could you do that**!**
Use **exclamation points** after single words to express enthusiasm, surprise, disbelief or intense emotion.	**Examples:** • **Congratulations!** You won**!** • **Yes!** I'm engaged**!** • **Oh!** I didn't expect that**!**
Use **exclamation points** after **repeated words** that are used for emphasis.	**Example:** • **Going! Going!** Our sale is almost over**!**

Italics

Main Titles and Subtitles Italicize the **main title** AND the **subtitle** of full-length, published books, and other creative compositions. You may also underline longer, published works.	**Examples:** • *Revolting Bodies: The Struggle to Redefine Fat Identity* • *Can I Get a Witness?: Black Women and Depression* • *Desire: The Journey We Must Take to Find the Life God Offers*
Creative Works Italicize the names of full-length, **published** creative, literary, periodical, and musical compositions when citing them within sentences.	**Examples:** • **Books:** *The Bluest Eye* • **Magazines:** *Newsweek* • **Newspapers:** *USA Today* • **Plays:** *A Raisin in the Sun* • **Music:** *Too Legit to Quit*

Italics *(Cont'd)*

Words in a Series

When writing a **list** of items that require italics, you must also **italicize** the **punctuation** that encloses or follows (*e.g. commas, colons, quotation marks*).

Examples:

*   After reading ***The Words You Should Know to Sound Smart,*** Alex decided to include *ennui*, *largess,* and *insouciant* in his daily vocabulary to the annoyance of his close friends and family.

Foreign Words

Italicize **foreign words** and **phrases** that are not considered part of the English language.

*The phrase *nouveau riche* is commonly used in American media and pop culture and may or may not be italicized.

Examples:

*   The **nouveau riche** often become *non compos mentis* when faced with gaining so much money so quickly, and frequently purchase expensive, unnecessary material goods.

Defining Words

When writing **formal definitions**, use *italics* to highlight the word that is being defined.

Examples:

*   The Italian term ***ciao*** derives from ***schiavo,*** "I am your slave."

Special Letters

Use **italics** for **alphabet letters** that are included in special phrases or mathematical equations.

Examples:

*   Stay on your p's and q's.
*   Solve for x when y = 6.
*   Dot your i's and cross your t's.

Parentheses

Use **parentheses** to enclose (nonessential) information that relates to its surrounding text.	**Examples:** • The illustration **(see page 94)** is very important.
Parentheses signal **"by the way"** to the reader.	• Marion doesn't feel **(and why should he)** like teaching the disruptive class.

Periods

Sentences Always end a **complete sentence** with a period.	**Examples:** • Gary ironed his suit**.** • Oliver fed his newborn daughter and fell asleep**.**
Numbers Use **periods** as **decimal points** in numerical expressions.	**Examples:** • **88.5** degrees • **$15.95** per unit
Abbreviations (Academic Degrees) Use **periods** when abbreviating academic **degrees** or proper names.	**Examples:** • Margaret Taylor, **Ph.D.** • **A. D.** Hall
Abbreviations (Titles) Use **periods** with **titles** and lower case abbreviations.	**Examples:** • Mr., Mrs., Jr., Sr., Rev. • a.m., p.m., etc., vol.
Use **periods** with some uppercase and mixed case abbreviations.	• U.S., A.D., B.C., Ph.D., Ave., St., Co., Oct., Fri.

Periods *(Cont'd)*

Inside Parentheses If the phrase inside the **parenthesis** is a complete sentence **(independent clause),** put the period **inside** the parenthesis.	**Examples:** • Tammy feels woozy. **(Her head hurts.)** • Soup is on sale. **(Chicken noodle is the best flavor.)**
Outside Parentheses If the phrase inside the **parenthesis** is **NOT** a complete sentence, put the period **outside** the parenthesis.	**Example:** • Tammy felt some strange symptoms yesterday **(dizziness and shoulder pains).**

Question Marks

Question marks end sentences written as questions or inquiries.	**Examples:** • Where are my glasses**?** • Did you pack your shoes**?** Your socks**?**

Quotation Marks

Dialogue Use **quotation marks** to indicate **direct quotes** or dialogue.	**Example:** • Manuel asked the interviewer, **"What is the starting salary?"**
Titles of Creative Works Use **quotation marks** to indicate **titles** of short works: speeches, sermons, magazines, essays, plays, films, brochures, songs, poems, articles, chapters, reports, events, lectures, or unpublished works.	**Example:** • Have you read my speech **"The Power of Reputation?"** • The poem **"Now"** by Audre Lorde is short and powerful.

Quotation Marks *(Cont'd)*

Technical Terms Use **quotation marks** for **technical terms** used in non-standard ways.	**Example:** • **"Content curation"** simply means picking stuff off the internet to share.
Special Emphasis Use **quotation marks** to emphasize or to *air-quote* certain words.	**Example:** • Shar **"experimented"** a lot in her college days.
With Punctuation **Periods** and **commas** are placed **inside** the closing quotation marks. **Colons** and **semicolons** are placed **outside** closing quotation marks. **Question marks** and **exclamation points** can appear **inside** or **outside** closing quotation marks.	**Examples:** • "I wanted**,**" Lucetta said, "to finish this meeting on time**."** • The following animals are considered **"marsupials"**: kangaroo, koala, and opossum. • **"How are you?!"** Betty yelled. • Have you read the report, **"Successful Start-up Businesses"**?
Special Expressions Use **quotation marks** to set off special expressions.	**Examples:** • New York is often called **"The Big Apple."** • Chicago is **"The Windy City."**

Semicolons

- **Semicolons** create a stronger break than a comma.

- **Semicolons** are used for separation and division.

- **Semicolons** connect short sentences.

Use a **semicolon** to connect two **independent clauses (complete sentences)** that are related in meaning, but not joined by a conjunction.	**Examples:** • Operations tripled productivity in the first **quarter;** marketing doubled in revenue. • Margarine costs less than **butter;** it contains less saturated fat.
Use a **semicolon** in a **list** of items that contain commas. The **semicolon** separates each individual item to reduce confusion.	**Examples:** • The officers of the school board are John Robinson, President; Susan Tate, Vice-President; Becky Feeny, Treasurer; James Jackson, Secretary; and Jan Jenkins, Historian.
Use a **semicolon** when joining **two independent clauses** with transitional expressions such as: • consequently • however • nevertheless • therefore	**Examples:** • Ruth dealt with difficult customers effectively; **consequently,** we forwarded all the tough calls to her extension.

Punctuation Exercise

Directions: Insert the correct punctuation for each sentence below. Some sentences require more than one punctuation mark.

1. Are we there yet she asked

2. Everyones going to Sashas for dinner at eight.

3. Mix the oil and vinegar at a 1 2 ratio.

4. I hope I get a lot of presents today is my birthday.

5. Stop talking to me

6. My little sister is 10 years old

7. By the way your dad called about an hour ago.

8. Ayanna my supervisor was born September 9 1981.

9. You need these items for the cookie recipe salt sugar and flour.

10. Mr. Stackhouses daughter is wearing earbuds and cant hear you.

Answers: Punctuation Exercise

1. **"Are we there yet?"** she asked**.**

2. **Everyone's** going to **Sasha's** for dinner at eight.

3. Mix the oil and vinegar at a **1:2** ratio.

4. I hope I get a lot of **presents;** today is my birthday.   **OR**

   I hope I get a lot of **presents:** today is my birthday.

5. Stop talking to me**!**

6. My little sister is 10 years old**.**

7. By the way**,** your dad called about an hour ago.

8. Ayanna**,** my supervisor**,** was born September 9**,** 1981.

9. You need these items for the cookie recipe**:** salt**,** sugar **and** flour. **OR**

   You need these items for the cookie recipe**:** salt**,** sugar**,** and flour.

10. Mr. **Stackhouse's** daughter is wearing earbuds and **can't** hear you.

Chapter Fourteen
Numbers

Photo Credit: Canstock Photos, nakophotography.

When to Write Numbers as Words

In many cases, determining when to use words or numerals is easy, but others are a bit tricky to remember, especially when writing or editing longer technical documents. Accurately proofreading for numbers also involves punctuation, as many numerical expressions incorporate commas, periods, and colons. These rules in this chapter are based on William A. Sabin's *The Gregg Reference Manual 11th edition*, which is more popular among business writers, but generally acceptable across most style guides. In general, if you want to emphasize numbers or statistics, use numerals, but if not, use words. If you have a style preference, aside from the rules, then remember to remain consistent in presenting numbers as numerals or as words from sentence to sentence. Check your style guide for preferences regarding numbers.

Rule #1: Spell out numbers one through nine.

Examples:

- Anita bought **nine** boxes of blue pens and **five** cases of copy paper last month.

- Little Robbie turns **two** this Saturday.

Rule #2: Spell out numbers that begin a sentence.

Examples:

- **Seven hundred** staff workers were cut from public schools statewide.

- **Thirty-five** people enrolled in our grant writing class.

Rule #3: Spell out ordinal numbers that end with *-nd, -rd, -st, or –th* that can be expressed in one or two words. Remember, hyphenated numbers count as one word.

Examples:

- The marketing team celebrated Charlie's **twenty-third** work anniversary.

- Remember the **twentieth** century?

Rule #4: Spell out numbers ten or less in street names. However, use figures for numbers greater than ten within street names. Remember, this rule does not apply to the location's building or suite number, unless a particular situation calls for extreme formality in writing addresses solely with words, as with wedding invitations or proclamations.

Examples:

- Keith moved his office from **One** Capitol Ave. to 1121 **Third** St.
- 185 **Second** Avenue
- 1908 West **65th** Street

Rule #5: Spell out exact or approximate numbers that consist of two words or hyphenated numerical expressions.

> **Examples:**
>
> - **three hundred** guests   **one-half** of voters
> - **sixty-odd** volunteers   **thirty-three million** followers

Rule #6: Spell out fractions that do not contain whole numbers. However, use numbers if the fraction is long or awkward when written in words.

> **Examples:**
> - **two-thirds** of the class
> - **one-quarter** of a mile
> - **3/4-yard** lengths (instead of **three-quarter** yard lengths)

Rule #7: Spell out ages not followed by *years* or *months* old.

> **Examples:**
>
> - My mother turns **sixty-seven** this year.
> - Celia still feels sexy at **seventy**.

Rule #8: Spell out numbers in expressions of time, if the numbers are followed by the phrase *o'clock,* or if the numbers stand alone.

> **Examples:**
> - Sam will meet us for lunch at **eleven o'clock**.
> - Dr. Hampton dismissed class at **eight** instead of **nine**.

Rule #9: When writing money values, use cents to spell out numbers less than one dollar.

> **Examples:**
> - Maurice paid **seventy-five** cents for a candy bar.
> - The cashier owed me **forty-seven** cents in change.

Rule #10: Spell out numbers **twenty-one (21)** through **ninety-nine (99)**. Be sure to include the hyphen.

Examples:

- **Twenty-five** hundred balloons
- **Forty-seven** thousand and five dollars

Rule #11: Spell out numbers in dates when the day is expressed in ordinal numbers **before** the month.

Examples:

- We left on the **third** of **August**.
- Trisha starts her new job on the **tenth** of **June**, but her mother retires on the **first** of **July**.

When to Use Numbers (Not Words)

Rule #1: For numbers ten or higher, use numerals.

Examples:

- Rita bought **10 boxes** of toner and **15 boxes** of paper clips.
- Charles bought **20 bouquets** of flowers for his wedding anniversary.

Rule #2: Use numerals when writing a series of items.

Examples:

- The food bank still needs **200** turkeys, **30** cans of green beans, and **25** bags of rolls for Thanksgiving dinner.

- Our elementary teachers need **20** packs of pencils, **25** rolls of paper towels, and **15** reams of copy paper.

Rule #3: Use numerals in front of the word millions or billions.

Examples:

- Oprah Winfrey is worth **2.9 billion** dollars.
- The lottery jackpot now totals **1.5 million** dollars.

Rule #4: In street names, write numbers 10 or higher as numerals, including ordinal numbers.

    Examples:

- The office settled at **16** East **31st** St. instead of **1404** S. Main St.
- Take a left at **125th** and Cross Street.

Rule #5: Use numbers for mixed fractions with whole numbers.

    Examples:

- Ginger's 12-year-old daughter now wears an **8 ½** size women's shoe.
- You need **2 ½** pounds of butter for this pound cake recipe.

Rule #6: Use numbers in expressions of time followed by a.m., p.m., noon or midnight. In general, delete *:00* from on the hour expressions of time.

    Examples:

- **8 a.m.** sales meeting **(not 8:00 a.m.)**

- **12 noon** lunch

- **1 p.m.** webinar

- **12 Midnight** chat

Rule #7: Use cardinal (regular) numbers in dates when the **day** comes **after** the **month.** However, when the **day** comes **before** the **month,** use ordinal numbers that end with the letters *-nd, -rd, -st,* or *–th*.

    Examples:

- Lucy graduated college **May 18, 1996**.

- **May 31** is my birthday.

- Summer camp runs **June 25-July 6.**

- Tuesday, the **7th of April**

Rule #8: Use numbers to express percentages and decimals.

    Examples:

- Dr. Ross's department paid **35%** of the training bill totaling **$2,565.82.**

- After the fundraiser, **40%** of the proceeds will be donated to the local library.

Rule #9: Use numbers to express whole dollars and cents over .00. It is not necessary to include zero cents after whole numbers ($300, not $300.00).

> **Examples:**

- the invoice for **$1,500.75**   my **$450** freelance editing fee

Rule #10: Use numbers to express feet, inches, pounds, and degree.

> **Examples:**

- **50 pounds** of wood
- **8 by 10** feet
- **180-degree** turn

- **20-mile** radius
- **2 1/2** inches
- **80°F**

Rule #11: Use numbers for ordinals longer than one or two words.

> **Examples:**

- One hundred and thirty first = **131st**
- **220th** in line
- **133rd** & Weston
- **109th** Congress

Rule #12: Use numbers to express compound or descriptive time frames.

> **Examples:**

- **8-hour** day
- **30-year** mortgage
- **3-day** seminar
- **15-year** marriage

Numbers Exercise

Directions: Make all necessary changes to expressions of numbers.

To: Tony R. Daniels
From: Carol E. Fisher
Subject: Formal Disciplinary Hearings Scheduled for July 10th-13th

The agency's calendar for July includes the dates of July 10th, 11th, 12th, and 13th for formal disciplinary hearings. Because of the length of time of hearings each day (8:00 a.m.-6:00 p.m.), we are having problems securing hotel space for the hearings. Most of the hotels we have contacted will only commit the meeting space from 9:00 a.m. to 5:00 p.m.

Yesterday my administrative assistant contacted the Joe C. Thompson Conference Center on 4455 3rd Street in Austin to determine whether it had suitable space available for July 10th-13th. She indicated that they had a meeting room one hundred fifty feet by fifty feet that is available. There is also no restriction on time limit for use of the room if we conclude the hearings by 7:00 p.m. each day.

The 1 problem I see is that eighty students from the University of Houston College of Pharmacy may want to attend 2 days of the hearings. Since this room can only accommodate 30-odd members of the class, I suggest we videotape the hearings. The other fifty can view the selected hearings at a later date.

Since the agency does not own the equipment to videotape the proceedings, I would suggest that we contract for this service. 4 vendors are available, but 2 of the 4 bids look the most attractive. *Audio-Visual Productions* has quoted $350.00 for 1 eight-hour hearing, and *Sound Systems* has quoted $349.50. Each requires 1/4 of the total amount as a deposit.

Since time is running short, please contact me by Friday, the 15th of May, so that I can brief you on the specific cases that will be heard in July. If you need to discuss this matter with me on May 6th or 7th, I will be in Washington, D.C. at the Fairmont Hotel, 2 Lexington Avenue, (202)-961-3500.

Answers: Numbers Exercise

To: Tony R. Daniels
From: Carol E. Fisher
Subject: Formal Disciplinary Hearings Scheduled for July **10-13**

The agency's calendar for July includes the dates of July **10, 11, 12,** and **13** for formal disciplinary hearings. Because of the length of time of hearings each day (**8** a.m.-**6** p.m.), we are having problems securing hotel space for the hearings. Most of the hotels we have contacted will only commit the meeting space from **9** a.m. to **5** p.m.

Yesterday my administrative assistant contacted the Joe C. Thompson Conference Center on 4455 **Third** Street in Austin to determine whether it had suitable space available for July **10-13**. She indicated that they had a meeting room **150 by 50 feet** that is available. There is also no restriction on time limit for use of the room if we conclude the hearings by **7 p.m.** each day.

The **one** problem I see is that **80** students from the University of Houston College of Pharmacy may want to attend **two** days of the hearings. Since this room can only accommodate **thirty-odd** members of the class, I suggest we videotape the hearings. The other **50** can view the selected hearings at a later date.

Since the agency does not own the equipment to videotape the proceedings, I would suggest that we contract for this service. **Four** vendors are available, but **two** of the **four** bids look the most attractive. *Audio-Visual Productions* has quoted **$350** for **one 8-hour** hearing, and *Sound Systems* has quoted $349.50. Each requires **one-fourth** of the total amount as a deposit.

Since time is running short, please contact me by Friday, the 15th of May, so that I can brief you on the specific cases that will be heard in July. If you need to discuss this matter with me on May **6** or **7**, I will be in Washington, D.C. at the Fairmont Hotel, **Two** Lexington Avenue, (202)-961-3500.

Chapter Fifteen
Noun-Pronoun Agreement

Photo Credit: Thinkstock Photos, Jupiterimages.

What is Noun-Pronoun Agreement?

A **noun** and its **pronoun** must agree in person, number and gender, whether they act as the subject of a sentence, object of a verb, object of a preposition, or as a possessor (owner) of items.

Examples:

- ***Shannon*** wants to know whether ***her*** proposal has been accepted.

- The grand ***jury*** has completed ***its*** investigation.

- *I* must support ***my*** client, as ***you*** must support ***yours***.

Rule #1: **Singular nouns** must be matched with **singular pronouns** to achieve agreement within the sentence.

Examples:

- **Gregory** researched **his** New Orleans family roots.

- **You** must pay **your** own tuition fees.

- **Aswan** released **her** barriers to love and got engaged.

Rule #2: **Plural nouns** must be matched with **plural pronouns** to achieve agreement within the sentence.

Examples:

- **Deborah and Jean** left **their** bibles at church.

- Rickey baked **cakes** and sold **them** to local diners.

- The **football players** lost, but **they** ate pizza after the game.

Rule #3: When a pronoun refers to nouns joined by **or**, **nor**, **either/or**, **neither/nor**, or **not only/but also**, and one of the nouns is plural, make the pronoun match the noun that is positioned closest to the verb or the last noun before the conjunction.

Examples:

- **Either** Dan **or Terry (singular noun)** will have to give up **his (singular pronoun)** office.

- **Neither** Tara **nor** her **daughters (plural noun)** asked **their (plural pronoun)** husbands for money.

- **Not only** the executive assistants, **but also** the **manager (singular noun)** needs to turn in **his or her (singular pronoun)** timecard by Friday afternoon.

Types of Pronouns

Nominative Pronouns: Function as subjects; also called "naming" pronouns.	• I, he, she, we, • who, you, they, it
Objective Pronouns: Function as objects of verbs or prepositions.	• me, him, her, us, them, whom, you, it
Possessive Pronouns: Show ownership; no apostrophes.	• my/mine, his, her/hers, our/ours, their/theirs, whose, your/yours, its

Ready to test your grammar skills?

Challenge your grammar and editing prowess with the book **Proofreading Power Skills & Drills,** and the online class. Visit the websites below for more information.

Ordering information:

www.arhampton.com/classes
www.arhampton.com/books

Knowledge Check

Directions: Change the number in parentheses to the correct cardinal expression.

1. Lana is sitting in the **(4)** _____row.

2. Mrs. Lee was born on the **(25)** _____day of January.

3. We are going on our **(3)** _____date.

4. Brenden scored in the **(99)** _____percentile.

5. Dr. Gore was the **(1000)** _____radio caller who won a prize.

6. That was Jill's **(10)** _____prank phone call today.

7. Christopher's birthday was the **(21)** _____of August.

Answers: 1. fourth 2. twenty-fifth 3. third 4. ninety-ninth 5. one thousandth 6. tenth 7. twenty-first

Noun-Pronoun Exercise

Directions: Choose and circle the correct **pronouns** to fill in the blanks.

1. Neither Jack nor Bill remembered to bring_____membership card to the gym.

    a. his   **b. their**   **c. they're**

2. One of the hotel guests left_____purse on the couch in the lobby.

    a. his or her   **b. their**   **c. she**

3. At the concert hall,_____said that I could leave Donna's ticket at the box office.

    a. him   **b. they**   **c. we**

4. Jonathan and_____thought that skydiving might be fun to try.

    a. I   **b. me**   **c. her**

5. Everyone must bring_____own chair to the outdoor jazz concert.

    a. their   **b. our**   **c. his or her**

6. The cab driver told Vic and_____that traffic on the bridge was heavy at this time of day.

    a. me   **b. I**   **c. myself**

7. The company launched_____new environmental campaign today.

    a. their   **b. it's**   **c. its**

Answers: Pronoun Exercise

1. **(a)** his

2. **(a)** his or her

3. **(b)** they

4. **(a)** I

5. **(c)** his or her

6. **(a)** me

7. **(c)** its

Chapter Sixteen
Abbreviations

Photo Credit: Picography, Burst.

What are Abbreviations?

Abbreviations are groups of letters resulting from shortening a word by removing letters or by using the first few letters of a word.

There are **two types of abbreviations**: acronyms and initialisms.

Examples:

- Avenue—**Ave.**
- Doctor—**Dr.**
- Road—**Rd.**
- Street—**St.**

What are Acronyms?

A phrase formed from the first letters of a group of words; usually capitalized.

The **acronym** often sounds like a regular word when pronounced.

Examples:
- AIDS
- RADAR
- LASER
- SCUBA
- UNICEF

Entire Word	Abbreviation
Acquired Immune Deficiency Syndrome	• AIDS
Radio Detection and Ranging	• RADAR
Light Amplification by Stimulated Emission of Radiation	• LASER
Self-Contained Underwater Breathing Apparatus	• SCUBA
United Nations International Children's Emergency Fund	• UNICEF

What are Initialisms?

A phrase formed from the first letters of a group of words; usually capitalized.

In **initialisms**, each letter is spoken individually and does not create a regular word.

Examples:
- CEO
- NAACP
- BBC
- UK
- UN

Entire Word	Abbreviation
Chief Executive Officer	• CEO
National Association for the Advancement of Colored People	• NAACP
British Broadcasting Corporation	• BBC
United Kingdom	• UK
United Nations	• UN

Abbreviations Exercise

Directions: Does the sentence below contain an **abbreviation**, **acronym** or **initialism**? Circle only **ONE** best answer.

1. Kevin's dating profile says he likes TV, movies, and long walks.

   abbreviation   **acronym**   **initialism**

2. Are you a fan of WNBA games?

   abbreviation   **acronym**   **initialism**

3. Martin refused to SCUBA dive on his Hawaiian vacation.

   abbreviation   **acronym**   **initialism**

4. The marketing team recorded the client's PSA under budget.

   abbreviation   **acronym**   **initialism**

5. Renaye's oldest child was born Sept. 2, 2002.

   abbreviation   **acronym**   **initialism**

6. Please attach the photo as a JPG instead of a PNG.

   abbreviation   **acronym**   **initialism**

7. Is Dr. Vaughn available to meet this afternoon?

   abbreviation   **acronym**   **initialism**

Answers: Abbreviations Exercise

1. initialism

2. initialism

3. acronym

4. initialism

5. abbreviation

6. acronym

7. abbreviation

Chapter Seventeen
Prepositions

Photo Credit: Unsplash, Green Chameleon.

What are Prepositions?

Prepositions are function words that show relationship between subjects, objects, and other parts of a sentence. Prepositions also describe location or position by showing where or in relation to what (e.g., *above* or *behind*).

In addition to spatial relationships, prepositions also clarify time or temporal (time) relationships with words like "before" or "after." A preposition must also have an object—a noun or a pronoun—following it. This noun or pronoun is called the **object of the preposition**.

A **prepositional phrase** is the **combination** of the **preposition** and the **object** that follows. Prepositional phrases add description and detail to otherwise complete sentences. Even if these prepositional phrases are deleted, a complete sentence should remain. However, the remaining short sentence might lack important details without the prepositional phrase.

Examples:

- The dance studio sits **behind the Walgreens on Main Street**.
- Sylvia left her purse **in the restaurant**.
- Donnie left **without saying goodbye**.

Ending Sentences with Prepositions

Contrary to popular belief and long-standing American language customs, **you can end a sentence with a preposition**. This should not be counted as a grammatical error, but rather a questionable choice of writing style.

Although you want to avoid doing so in formal essays or reports, it is acceptable for the casual speaker or the casual writer to end a statement or question with a preposition.

If a sentence sounds awkward or strange in attempts to avoid ending it with a preposition, just use the preposition. You can also reword the sentence altogether. However, for high-stakes documents in formal business or educational settings, **it is best to avoid ending sentences with prepositions**.

Common Prepositions

about	by	off	until
after	during	on	up
against	except	out	with
among	for	over	within
before	from	since	
behind	in	than	
beside	into	through	
between	of	to	

Prepositions Exercise

Directions: Cross out all **prepositional phrases** in the sentences below.

1. Rosalyn became a successful corporate accountant in spite of her traumatic childhood.

2. Perry always meditates before writing a sermon.

3. Braylon hid his favorite cookies behind the microwave.

4. One of Carla's extensions fell out of her hair during our cardio kick boxing class.

5. A generous client sent Stephen an expensive bottle of wine for landing a huge contract.

6. Nina should have checked the weather reports before washing her car.

7. Many bank tellers cannot tell the difference between a fake $100 bill and a real one.

Answers: Prepositions Exercise

1. Rosalyn became a successful corporate accountant ~~**in spite of her traumatic childhood**~~.

2. Perry always meditates ~~**before writing a sermon**~~.

3. Braylon hid his favorite cookies ~~**behind the microwave**~~.

4. One ~~**of Carla's extensions**~~ fell ~~**out of her hair during our cardio kick boxing class**~~.

5. A generous client sent Stephen an expensive bottle ~~**of wine for landing a huge contract**~~.

6. Nina should have checked the weather reports ~~**before washing her car**~~.

7. Many bank tellers cannot tell the difference ~~**between a fake $100 bill and a real one**~~.

Chapter Eighteen
Proofreading Challenge

Photo Credit: Unsplash, Nik MacMillan.

Proofreading Exercises

Now, it is time to test your knowledge! The following pages contain exercises that assess your proofreading abilities. The answers follow each exercise.

Online Classes & Resources

If you want in-depth, self-paced video training classes to quickly improve your professional writing skills, visit our website, and enroll in our affordable online classes. We also accommodate groups and teams for organizations that see the value in boosting employee writing skills.

www.arhampton.com

Onyx Online Education & Training Courses

Grammar Essentials Jump-start

Good writing starts with good grammar! **"Grammar Essentials Jump-start"** is jam-packed with useful information to help improve your grammar knowledge and build confidence in your writing skills.

Business Grammar Bootcamp

"Business Grammar Bootcamp" goes beyond general grammar. This class is the most comprehensive and cost-effective online course for quickly improving your knowledge of grammar and usage in workplace writing.

Public Speaking Skills for Everyday Success

Does speaking in front of groups of people make you nervous? **"Public Speaking Skills for Everyday Success"** offers valuable tips and techniques on how to deliver effective speeches and oral presentations.

Proofreading Power

"Proofreading Power" provides the fundamentals of proofreading through practical exercises and quizzes. You must have strong grammar skills to successfully complete this course. Also, order your copy of *Proofreading Power: Skills & Drills* to reinforce your learning.

Smarty Pants Vocabulary Builders

Have you ever wanted to sound smart? At some point, all of us want to use *'fancy'* words to convey our deepest most intelligent thoughts. In **"Smarty Pants Vocabulary Builders,"** you will upgrade your vocabulary with French, Latin, German and Italian words and phrases.

Agenda Exercise

Directions: Find and correct **six (6) errors** in this sample agenda.

Meeting of ad hoc Committee on Communication:
June 20, 2018

AGENDA

1. Welcome/Introductions

2. Minutes of last mateing

3. PR update

4. Employee sociale media posts

5. Department cancerns

6. Internal communication overview

7. External communnication rules

8. New busyness

9. Additional concerns

10.   Datte of next meeting

Answers: Agenda Exercise

Meeting of ad hoc Committee on Communication:
June 20, 2018

AGENDA

1. Welcome/Introductions

2. Minutes of last **meeting**

3. PR update

4. Employee **social** media posts

5. Department **concerns**

6. Internal communication overview

7. External **communication** rules

8. New **business**

9. Additional concerns

10.   **Date** of next meeting

Email Exercise

Directions: Find and correct **seven (7) errors** in this email.

To: The Sales Department

Subject: Quarterly Sales Figures

After compleating my analysis of the latest sales figures, the results show an overall increase of 5% over the previous quarter.

Sells of menswear were slightly down, but this was more than compensated for by increases in women's clothing. Our *value-for-money* range of women's winter boolts performed particularly well.

These results are satisfactory, given the difficult economic climate. However, we need to do better if we are to withstand the competition. In particular, I beleive there is substantial opportunity for increasing high-quality leisure footwear for children and young adults. This is a important market, and one which continues to see strong growth. I would therefore like everyone to make speciale efforts to promode these products.

Grace Kelly
Sales Manager

Answers: Email Exercise

To: The Sales Department

Subject: Quarterly Sales Figures

After **completing** my analysis of the latest sales figures, the results show an overall increase of 5% over the previous quarter.

Sales of menswear were slightly down, but this was more than compensated for by increases in women's clothing. Our *value-for-money* range of women's winter **boots** performed particularly well.

These results are satisfactory, given the difficult economic climate. However, we need to do better if we are to withstand the competition. In particular, I **believe** there is substantial opportunity for increasing high-quality leisure footwear for children and young adults. This is **an** important market, and one which continues to see strong growth. I would therefore like everyone to make **special** efforts to **promote** these products.

Grace Kelly
Sales Manager

Resignation Letter Exercise

Directions: Find **12 errors** in this sample resignation letter.

Tina Jeffers

2525, Maple Drive

Anywhere, USA 77777

ABC Financial Services
7779311 Portland Aveanue
Anywhere, USA 99999

Friday July 20, 20018

Dear Human Resources:

Please except this letter as notification that I am laveing my position with ABC Financial Services effective immedately.

Thanks you for the opportunities you have provided me during my time with the company. I am more than greatful to have worked with the teem hear.

Sincierely,

Tina Jeffers

Tina Jeffers
Collections Analyst

Answers: Resignation Letter

Tina Jeffers
2525 Maple Drive
Anywhere, USA 77777

ABC Financial Services
7779311 Portland **Avenue**
Anywhere, USA 99999

Friday, July 20, **2018**

Dear Human Resources:

Please **accept** this letter as notification that I am **leaving** my position
with ABC Financial Services effective **immediately**.

Thank you for the opportunities you have provided me during my time with the
company. I am more than **grateful** to have worked with the **team here**.

Sincerely,

Tina Jeffers

Tina Jeffers
Collections Analyst

More Resources from

Ashan R. Hampton

B & W Print - **ISBN:** 978-0-359-69282-8

Adult Learner Grammar Essentials teaches you to effectively correct the most common grammar errors encountered in academic and professional writing. With self-study quizzes and plain English explanations, you will improve your grammar skills in just minutes a day. Upon completing the pre-test and post-test, and all the exercises in between, you will clearly understand how to apply good grammar usage to your everyday writing assignments.

Ordering information:

www.arhampton.com/books

B & W Print - **ISBN:** 978-1-721-95551-0

Can you catch mistakes in your own writing? Do you know how to identify and correct common writing errors? Would you like to become an effective proofreader for personal growth or profit? *Proofreading Power: Skills & Drills* provides essential rules, guidelines and tips to quickly boost your editing prowess. Train yourself to catch mistakes in the smallest of details with practical exercises on grammar, mechanics, usage, punctuation and spelling.

Ordering information:

www.arhampton.com/books

References

Associated Press. *The Associated Press Stylebook 2020-2022*. 55th Edition. New York: Basic Books. 2020. Print.

Loberger, Gordon and Kate Shoup. *Webster's New World English Grammar Hand Book*. 2nd Edition. New York: Houghton Mifflin Harcourt, 2009. Print.

Sabin, William A. *The Gregg Reference Manual*. 11th Edition. New York: McGraw-Hill, 2011.

Index

Made in United States
North Haven, CT
18 March 2023

34165591R00083